Public Policy Issues Associated with the SAFRR Tsunami Scenario

Open-File Report 2013–1170–M
California Geological Survey Special Report 229

U.S. Department of the Interior
U.S. Geological Survey

The SAFRR (Science Application for Risk Reduction) Tsunami Scenario

Stephanie Ross and Lucile Jones, Editors

Public-Policy Issues Associated with the SAFRR Tsunami Scenario

By Laurie A. Johnson and Charles R. Real

Open-File Report 2013–1170–M

California Geological Survey Special Report 229

U.S. Department of the Interior
U.S. Geological Survey

U.S. Department of the Interior
SALLY JEWELL, Secretary

U.S. Geological Survey
Suzette M. Kimball, Acting Director

U.S. Geological Survey, Reston, Virginia 2013

For product and ordering information:
World Wide Web: http://www.usgs.gov/pubprod
Telephone: 1-888-ASK-USGS

For more information on the USGS—the Federal source for science about the Earth,
its natural and living resources, natural hazards, and the environment:
World Wide Web: http://www.usgs.gov
Telephone: 1-888-ASK-USGS

Suggested citation:
Johnson, L.A., and Real, C.R., 2013, Public-policy issues associated with the SAFRR tsunami scenario,
chap. M, *in* Ross, S.L., and Jones, L.M., eds., The SAFRR (Science Application for Risk Reduction)
Tsunami Scenario: U.S. Geological Survey Open-File Report 2013–1170, 39 p.,
http://pubs.usgs.gov/of/2013/1170/m/.

STATE OF CALIFORNIA
EDMUND G. BROWN JR.
GOVERNOR

THE NATURAL RESOURCES AGENCY
JOHN LAIRD
SECRETARY FOR RESOURCES

DEPARTMENT OF CONSERVATION
MARK NECHODOM
DIRECTOR

CALIFORNIA GEOLOGICAL SURVEY
JOHN G. PARRISH, Ph.D.
STATE GEOLOGIST

Contents

Tables

Public-Policy Issues Associated with the SAFRR Tsunami Scenario

By Laurie A. Johnson[1] and Charles R. Real[2]

Introduction

The SAFRR (Science Application for Risk Reduction) tsunami scenario simulates a tsunami generated by a hypothetical magnitude 9.1 earthquake that occurs offshore of the Alaska Peninsula (Kirby and others, 2013). In addition to the work performed by the authors on public-policy issues associated with the SAFRR tsunami scenario, this section of the scenario also reflects the policy discussions of the State of California's Tsunami Policy Work Group, a voluntary advisory body formed in October 2011, which operates under the California Natural Resources Agency (CNRA), Department of Conservation, and is charged with identifying, evaluating, and making recommendations to resolve issues that are preventing full and effective implementation of tsunami hazard mitigation and risk reduction throughout California's coastal communities. It also presents the analyses of plans and hazard policies of California's coastal counties, incorporated cities, and major ports performed by the staff of the California Geological Survey (CGS) and Lauren Prehoda, Office of Environmental and Government Affairs, California Department of Conservation. It also draws on the policy framework and assessment prepared for the ARkStorm Pacific Coast winter storm and catastrophic flooding (Topping and others, 2010). This chapter was peer-reviewed by Robert Olson, Robert Olson and Associates, and Martin Eskijian, consulting engineer.

Policymaking Overview

In the United States, public policymaking is the responsibility of elected bodies, such as city councils, State legislatures, and the U.S. Congress. Managers of cities, counties, and special districts, as well as regional, State and Federal agencies also participate in policymaking, helping conceptualize and create policies. The policymaking process tends to evolve in response to societal or community problems perceived by citizens, interest groups, and political leaders. A rational description of the policymaking process can be described as a cycle (Newell, 2004, p. 153) of:

- *Agenda setting*, when issues are brought to the attention of policymakers.
- *Policy formulation*, when options are considered and a course of action is adopted.
- *Implementation*, when adopted policies are put into action.
- *Evaluation*, when a policy assessment is performed and ways to modify or improve policies are provided.

---

[1] Laurie Johnson Consulting Research.
[2] California Geological Survey.

Within this cycle, this tsunami policy assessment largely corresponds with the agenda and policy formulation stages. However, as Birkland (1997) and others have aptly documented, policy agenda setting and policy transformations rarely occur in such a rational, staged way. For U.S. disaster policy, much of the formulation and implementation have occurred mostly during relatively brief periods of time—usually following disastrous events (Birkland, 1997; Birkland, 2006; Rubin, 2012). As Birkland advises, "a disaster can often do in an instant what years of interest group activity, policy entrepreneurship, advocacy, lobbying, and research may not be able to do" (Birkland, 2006, p. 5). This is what occurred in aftermath of the catastrophic 2004 Indian Ocean tsunami, when Congress passed the Tsunami Warning and Education Act of 2006—a key piece of Federal legislation aimed at strengthening the tsunami detection, warning, education, and preparedness efforts in the U.S. (U.S. Congress, 2005; U.S. Congress, 2006).

This policy assessment considers the priority issues raised by the SAFRR tsunami scenario, with particular emphasis on the modeled physical, social, and economic impacts on California's coastal communities, ports, and harbors. Issues of tsunami science, modeling techniques, and national tsunami forecasting are not major components of this assessment. The priority policy issues are organized around the basic functions of disaster management—mitigation and preparedness, response, and recovery—as well as risk awareness, which is a major behavioral factor in disaster management. In addition, this assessment also identifies overarching policy considerations and possible courses of action.

U.S. and California Tsunami and Disaster Management Policy Framework

In the United States, most governance and policymaking works as a shared system in which, according to May and Williams (1986, p. 21), "common or overlapping responsibilities are apportioned among layers of government." "Federal shared governance creates an intergovernmental partnership for which noteworthy decision-making power about program or regulatory design and/or operations is exercised by both those in the Federal Government and those in subnational governments" (May and Williams 1986, p. 21). In the modern U.S. disaster management system, local governments, special districts, and tribal governments have primary responsibility for supplying disaster-related resources; regional, State, and Federal agencies are to provide support as requested (Federal Emergency Management Agency [FEMA], 2005). This shared system is triggered from the "bottom-up." Local governments are aided as needed by States, and both are aided, in turn, by the Federal Government. By design, the system requires extensive coordination and cooperation among all levels of government, as well as the many private organizations involved in disaster management. It is also a system of incentives, in that States and localities are encouraged, but not required, to participate.

Table 1 generalizes the current disaster policy framework in the United States for the basic disaster management functions, combining preparedness and mitigation, and adding risk awareness, with an emphasis on tsunami-related policy. The fundamental roles and responsibilities of each level of public policymaking—Federal, State, regional, county, and localities, as well as the private sector, are briefly described.

The Federal Government is primarily responsible for the Nation's tsunami alert and warning system, providing response and recovery assistance following major disasters, promoting risk awareness and preparedness, and encouraging State, local, and private mitigation and preparedness efforts, in some cases through the use of incentives. Major Federal legislation and programs include the following:

· *Tsunami Warning and Education Act of 2006* designates the National Oceanographic and Atmospheric Agency (NOAA) through the National Weather Service (NWS) to provide continued

2

tsunami alert and notification responsibilities for a tsunami, generated anywhere in the world, that may impact U.S. States and territories. For the West Coast, including California, these alerts are issued by NOAA's West Coast and Alaska Tsunami Warning Center (WCATWC). The WCATWC has most of North America under its area of responsibility, whereas NOAA's Pacific Tsunami Warning Center (PTWC) provides alerts to the remainder of the Pacific Basin.

· *National Tsunami Hazard Mitigation Program (NTHMP)*. The NTHMP was first formed by Congressional action in 1995 and strengthened by the Tsunami Warning and Education Act of 2006. The NTHMP is a partnership between NOAA, the United States Geological Survey (USGS), the Federal Emergency Management Agency (FEMA), the National Science Foundation (NSF), and the 28 U.S. coastal States, territories, and commonwealths. It is focused on reducing the impact of tsunamis through hazard assessment, warning guidance, and mitigation (NOAA, 2013a). It also sets the standards for tsunami source identification, numerical modeling, and inundation and hazard mapping.

· *TsunamiReady Program* is led by the NWS at NOAA, and is part of the NTHMP. It is designed to help cities, towns, counties, universities, and other large sites in coastal areas reduce the potential for disastrous tsunami-related consequences (NOAA, 2013b). To be designated "TsunamiReady," a community must meet certain criteria for (1) communications and coordination, (2) receipt of tsunami warnings, (3) local warning dissemination, (4) preparedness, and (5) administration of a formal tsunami hazard operations plan. As of May 22, 2013, there were 144 TsunamiReady™ sites in 11 States, Puerto Rico, Guam and the Northern Mariana Islands, American Samoa, and one international site (NOAA, 2013b). Thirty-five of those sites are located in California, 21 of which are localities, seven are counties, three are government sites, two are Indian tribes, one is the University of California at Santa Barbara, and one is San Francisco airport. None of California's ports have been designated TsunamiReady, but some, such as the Port of Los Angeles, are located in cities or counties that have achieved this status.

· *National Response Framework (NRF)* is a guide to how the Nation responds to all types of disasters and emergencies (FEMA, 2013). It is built on scalable, flexible, and adaptable concepts identified in the National Incident Management System (NIMS) to align key roles and responsibilities across the country. The NRF describes specific authorities and best practices for managing response that include actions to save lives, protect property and the environment, stabilize communities, and meet basic human needs following an incident, as well as the execution of emergency plans and actions to support short-term recovery. Under the NRF, the Secretary of Homeland Security is the principal Federal official for domestic incident management and FEMA leads Federal response to incidents in which Federal assistance is provided under the Stafford Act.

· *Robert T. Stafford Disaster Relief and Emergency Assistance Act (Stafford Act)* provides for individual and household post-disaster assistance, Public Assistance grants to restore damaged public facilities and infrastructure, and mitigation grants that fund both local hazard mitigation planning and projects to help strengthen communities against future disaster losses (FEMA, 2007). Interacting with Stafford Act programs are the National Incident Management System (NIMS), which provides a standardized nationwide protocol for managing response at each level of government, and the NRF (FEMA, 2008) and the National Disaster Recovery Framework (FEMA 2011), which coordinate disaster response and recovery activities among Federal agencies.

· *National Disaster Recovery Framework (NDRF)* is a guide that enables effective recovery support to disaster-impacted States, tribes, and territorial and local jurisdictions (FEMA, 2011). It also defines a coordinating structure that can be activated and scaled as appropriate depending on the size and nature of the disaster and defines some key positions—Federal, State, and Tribal Disaster

Recovery Coordinators (FDRC, SDRC, and TDRC) and Local Disaster Recovery Managers (LDRMs)—as well as six recovery support functions (RSF)—community planning and capacity building, economic, health and social services, housing, infrastructure systems, and cultural and natural resources. FEMA is designated as the lead Federal agency to facilitate and coordinate RSF activities and recovery planning at the national level, and a series of RSF annexes further define the scope of each RSF and designate a Federal agency as the RSF coordinator along with a number of primary agencies and supporting organizations. The NDRF timeframe can extend for months, even years, following a major disaster.

- *U. S. Coast Guard* has incident response responsibility for the coastal zone, which includes all U.S. waters subject to tides, as well as specified ports and harbors. In tsunami response, the U.S. Coast Guard would provide mutual aid to the ports and affected jurisdictions statewide to support search and rescue operations, launch air support according to policy, notify commercial vessels and applicable facilities of a tsunami warning, close ports to all inbound vessel traffic and encourage vessels to move to a safe location, and conduct patrols of waterways within the affected zone to ensure maritime security.

- *Disaster Mitigation Act of 2000 (DMA 2000)* requires State and local adoption of FEMA-approved Hazard Mitigation Plans (HMP) as a precondition for receipt of Federal mitigation project grant funding. It also provides a competitive Pre-Disaster Mitigation (PDM) grant program to fund local hazard mitigation planning efforts and mitigation projects. Local HMPs typically contain maps showing areas of potential natural hazards, as well as a discussion of historic occurrences, an assessment of exposure and risk to infrastructure, proposed policies to mitigate the impact of future occurrences, and an Action Plan that must indicate priorities for mitigation activities that become formally adopted by the local governing body. Mitigation actions are commonly evaluated and prioritized using a tool from FEMA that evaluates strengths, weaknesses, opportunities, and constraints of proposed actions through a series of questions considering the following aspects: (1) social (community acceptance and effect of differing segments of population), (2) technical (feasibility, long-term solution, secondary impacts), (3) administrative (staffing requirements, funding needs, necessary maintenance and operations), (4) political (necessary support, local champion, public support), (5) legal (State authority, existing local authority, potential for legal challenge), and (6) economic (expected benefit, cost of implementation, contribution to economic goals, outside funding needs).

- *National Flood Insurance Program (NFIP)* provides flood insurance through the private sector, with backing by the Federal Government. Insurance is also reinforced by 100-year and 500-year floodplain mapping, together with rate reductions in relation to local government mitigation actions. Various types of flood mitigation and project grants are also administered. Tsunami losses are covered under the NFIP. However, the Flood Insurance Rate Maps (FIRMs) do not, as of yet, model tsunami risk as part of coastal flood mapping. The program requires communities to adhere to strict flood-resistant building codes in designated flood zones to qualify for the program. For coastal communities, such standards recognize hazards of coastal storm surge and hurricane-driven flood waters and provide specifications for building materials, design, and construction, which also help to provide resistance against low amplitude tsunami inundation. The NFIP represents the national position on "shared-risk." The Federal Government will help, but it aims to encourage local governments and individuals to share flood risk.

- *Coastal Zone Management Act of 1972* is administered by NOAA's Office of Ocean and Coastal Resource Management (OCRM) which works with States and territories to operate a system of National Estuarine Research Reserves, implement the National Coastal Zone Management (NCZM)

Program, and develop a system of marine protected areas. The NCZM program is a voluntary State-Federal partnership which encourages States to adopt their own management programs to meet the Federal goals of protection, restoration, and appropriate development of coastal zone resources. The OCRM has a modest annual budget that it primarily uses to match State funds for implementing resource improvements, enhancements, and pollution control in the designated coastal zone and national estuarine research reserves. The State of California is a participant in the NCZM Program and the California Coastal Commission and Bay Conservation and Development Commission are two designated State agencies responsible for developing and implementing the State's Coastal Zone Management Plan (CZMP).

The State of California participates in the national tsunami preparedness and risk awareness programs and also provides response and recovery assistance following major disasters, and encourages local and private mitigation and preparedness efforts, in some cases through the use of incentives. Major State legislation and programs include the following:

· *California Tsunami Preparedness and Hazard Mitigation Program (TPHMP)*. The program is funded by NOAA under the NTHMP and managed by the California Governor's Office of Emergency Services (Cal OES) with assistance from the California Geological Survey (CGS). It provides leadership and guidance, as well as financial support, for many tsunami preparedness, planning and hazard mitigation activities in the State. These include tsunami scenario modeling, preparation of tsunami inundation zone maps and evacuation zone maps, development and implementation of State and local emergency response and evacuation plans, tsunami-related exercises and training, and testing of the tsunami warning system. In 2009, the State TPHMP released a series of "Tsunami Inundation Maps for Emergency Planning," which have provided the basis for preparedness, planning, and education activities in California. These activities have including the preparation of evacuation and emergency response plans, production of multilanguage brochures, development and support of tsunami scenario-driven exercises and drills, development of workshops to educate both emergency managers and public, and establishment of a comprehensive information Web site (see *http://www.tsunami.ca.gov*), a preparedness Web site (see *http://myhazards.calema.ca.gov/*), and a Web service to assist in preparation of local hazard mitigation plans (see *http://myplan.calema.ca.gov/*). Activities are coordinated through the California Tsunami Steering Committee, comprised of representatives from the four regional NWS offices, all relevant State agencies, and each of the 20 coastal and San Francisco Bay area counties.

· *California Coastal Act of 1976*, established the California Coastal Commission (CCC) as an independent, quasi-judicial State agency to protect, conserve, restore, and enhance environmental and human-based resources of the California coast and ocean for use by current and future generations. The CCC, in partnership with the State's 60 coastal cities and 15 coastal counties, regulates the use of land and water in the coastal zone—an area specifically mapped by the California Legislature that varies in width from several hundred feet in highly urbanized areas to as much as 5 miles in certain rural areas and extends offshore in a 3-mile-wide band. The act requires all local governments within the coastal zone to develop local coastal plans (LCPs) that are then reviewed and certified by the CCC. Although the LCPs are primarily focused on environmental protection and public coastal access issues, these plans must also consider public safety issues. It is at this time that the CCC transfers permitting authority for most new development to the local government. The CCC retains appellate authority over development within 300 feet of the high tide line or the first public road, whichever is landward. About 90 percent of the State's coastal zone falls into an LCP. Development activities are broadly defined by the California Coastal Act to include (among others): construction of buildings, divisions of land, and activities that change the intensity of use of land or public access to coastal waters. These activities generally require a coastal permit from either the CCC or the local government. The Coastal Commission is one of California's two designated coastal-management agencies for the purpose of administering the Federal Coastal Zone Management Act. Following the 2011 Tohoku Oki tsunami in Japan, the California Coastal Commission added a requirement for the assessment of tsunami hazards for proposed development located in designated Coastal Zone and for recertification of LCPs. Most coastal counties and cities have not yet completed their LCP plan updates and the CCC's recertification process.

- *California State Lands Commission*, established in 1938, has jurisdiction over State lands, waterways, and resources. Public and private entities may apply to the commission for leases or permits to use, or conduct activities on, State lands for many purposes including marinas, industrial wharves, tanker anchorages, dredging, mining, and oil and gas (California State Lands Commission, 2013). For example, owners and developers of marinas along the State's bays are required to acquire a lease for use of the State's land at the marina site. The State Lands Commission also issues dredging permits to both public and private parties for work in harbors and waterways. After the 1994 Northridge earthquake, the State Lands Commission was funded through FEMA's Hazard Mitigation Grant Program (HMGP) to develop standards for marine oil terminals. In 2005, the Marine Oil Terminal Engineering and Maintenance Standards (MOTEMS) became an enforceable chapter in the California Building Code (chapter 31F), and more than 30 marine oil terminals along California's coast were mandated to comply with a comprehensive inspection program, along with updated requirements for mooring, berthing, seismic vulnerability and other mechanical systems. Mooring and berthing requirements have since been updated to consider the largest vessels calling at a terminal. Also, each marine oil terminal is now required to have a "tsunami plan," for shutting down operations, vacating the terminal, and doing whatever else is deemed necessary. Sea-level rise is also required to be considered under the standards.

- *Bay Conservation and Development Commission (BCDC)*, established by the McAteer-Petris Act of 1965, is the Federally designated State coastal-management agency for the San Francisco Bay segment of the California coastal zone. This designation empowers the commission to use the authority of the Federal Coastal Zone Management Act to ensure that Federal projects and activities are consistent with the policies of the San Francisco Bay Plan and State law. It is the only regional agency with any direct authority to regulate land use. BCDC issues permits for filling, dredging, and changes in use in San Francisco Bay, including salt ponds, managed wetlands, and the shoreline. BCDC makes these permitting decisions in concert with the policies in its long-term guidance document, the San Francisco Bay Plan, which, among other things, specifies which areas along the shoreline should be used for ports, recreation, wildlife refuges, and other purposes. BCDC's shoreline jurisdiction to regulate development only extends to 100 feet upland from the Bay. Local governments in the San Francisco Bay area have the most comprehensive authority over land use.

- *State Seismic Hazard Mapping Act of 1990* provides for a statewide seismic hazard mapping and technical advisory program to assist cities and counties in fulfilling their responsibilities to protect public health and safety by reducing and mitigating the effects of strong ground shaking, liquefaction, landslides, or other ground failure and other seismic hazards caused by earthquakes. The State Geologist, and thus the California Geological Survey, is charged with preparing the statewide maps and managing the technical advisory program. The act also directs cities and counties to take the seismic hazard map information into account in the preparation of the safety element of their general plans and in formulating land-use management policies and regulations. The act also requires the disclosure of State-specified natural hazards to prospective buyers of residential property at the time of sale. The act also explicitly states that the State Geologist may also map the potential effects of tsunami and seiche when information becomes available from other sources and the State Geologist determines the information is appropriate for use by local government.

·   *Safety element in local General Plans.* All counties and incorporated cities in California are required to prepare safety elements to be included in local General Plans (California Government Code Section 65302, subdivision (g)) and are subject to the requirement for consistency with the general plan of zoning, subdivision, and capital improvements decisions. The safety element must include mapping of known seismic and other geologic hazards, as well as flood hazard zones. It also must address evacuation routes, military installations, peak-load water supply requirements, and minimum road widths and clearances around structures, as those items relate to identified fire and geologic hazards. Cities and counties may adopt their local hazard mitigation plan (LHMP) as a part of the safety element of their general plans.

·   *California Oil Spill Prevention and Response Act of 1990,* led to the establishment of the Office of Oil Spill Prevention and Response (OSPR) in the California Department of Fish and Wildlife (CDFW) with primary authority to direct prevention, removal, abatement, response, containment, clean up, and mitigation of oil spills in the marine waters of California. The act created harbor safety committees for the harbors and adjacent regions of San Diego Bay; Los Angeles/Long Beach Harbor; Port Hueneme; San Francisco, San Pablo, and Suisun Bays; and Humboldt Bay. Committee membership is prescribed in the act and draws from the range of stakeholders—both public and private—involved with ports and harbors. Each harbor safety committee is required to plan "for the safe navigation and operation of vessels within its geographic region of responsibility . . . (by preparing a) . . . harbor safety plan which encompasses all vessel traffic within its region and addresses the region's unique safety needs" (State of California, 2005). Plans are required to address regional harbor conditions and include "existing and expected conditions of weather, tidal ranges, tidal currents (directions and velocities), and other factors which might impair or restrict visibility or impact vessel navigation" (State of California, 2005). The act also gave the State Lands Commission authorities over marine terminals.

·   *California Building Standards Code* is published in its entirety every 3 years by order of the California legislature, with supplements published in intervening years. The current code adopted in 2010 (California Code of Regulations, title 24, volume 1 of part 2) is derived in large part from the 2009 International Building Code (California Building Standards Commission, 2010). The California legislature also delegates authority to various State agencies, boards, commissions and departments to create building regulations to implement the State's statutes. These building regulations or standards have the force of law and take effect 180 days after their publication unless otherwise stipulated. A city, county, or city and county may establish more restrictive building standards reasonably necessary because of local climatic, geological, or topographical conditions. Findings of the local condition(s) and the adopted local building standard(s) must be filed with the California Building Standards Commission to become effective and may not be effective sooner than the effective date of the latest edition of California Building Standards Code.

In addition to these key policies programs, State and local emergency planning is guided by the Incident Command System (ICS)/Standardized Emergency Management System (SEMS) to coordinate response and recovery activities statewide. Counties serve as operational areas under the State's emergency response framework.

Table 1. Generalized framework for U.S. tsunami disaster policy.
[Adapted from Topping and others, 2010]

	Mitigation and Preparedness	Response	Recovery	Risk Awareness
Federal	Implement National Tsunami Hazard Mitigation Program (NTHMP) working with State-local agencies to improve tsunami detection, warning, preparedness and response, and including management of the TsunamiReady program. Manage Tsunami Warning Centers and Deep-Ocean Assessment and Report of Tsunamis (DART) sensor network. Require State-local adoption of Federal Emergency Management Agency (FEMA)-approved hazard mitigation plans for mitigation grant eligibility. Provide State-local pre- and post-disaster mitigation project grants. Provide Federally backed private flood insurance, 100- and 500-year floodplain maps, rate reductions linked to adoption of flood provisions in building codes other mitigation actions, and mitigation grants. Make building-site mitigation improvements reducing risks to Federal infrastructure.	Activate the national tsunami alert and warning system and dissemination protocols. Implement National Response Framework (NRF) and National Incident Management Systems (NIMS). Determine if a Presidential disaster declaration is warranted U.S. Coast Guard implements tsunami protocol of Planned Response overseeing port and harbor evacuation and maritime movements. Provide mutual aid and State and local assistance as requested Provide training and technical support for preparedness and response, including local response planning through the Tsunami Ready program. Establish and support communication and information mechanisms.	Provide State and local assistance to State and local governments, Indian tribes or authorized tribal organizations, and certain specified private nonprofit organizations for eligible emergency work and the repair, restoration, and replacement of damaged public facilities and infrastructure. Provide grant and loan assistance to individuals, families, and businesses for damages and economic losses. Provide limited resources for long-term recovery planning. Fund post-disaster mitigation to reduce future losses. Provide residential and commercial resources for recovery via the National Flood Insurance Program (NFIP).	Create and administer public education programs to promote risk awareness that work at a national level, and also fund State, regional, and locally specific efforts. Example: National Tsunami Preparedness Week. Provide limited funding for research and outreach on risk communication.

Table 1. Generalized framework for U.S. tsunami disaster policy.—Continued

[Adapted from Topping and others, 2010]

	Mitigation and Preparedness	Response	Recovery	Risk Awareness
State	Implement State Tsunami Hazard Mitigation Program (NTHMP) working with Federal-State-local agencies to improve tsunami detection, warning, preparedness and response. Prepare State Hazard Mitigation Plan. Require cities and counties to adopt general plans, including safety elements, Local Coastal Plans, and official hazard zones issued as part of the Seismic Hazard Mapping Act. Require cities and counties to approve developments consistent with general plans. Adopt the State building code and mandate local adoption and enforcement. Make building-site and infrastructure mitigation improvements reducing risks to State-owned facilities and infrastructure.	Initiate California State Warning Center (CSWC) as the designated Warning Point agency for dissemination of tsunami alerts and warnings. Implement State Emergency Plan framework and Standardized Emergency Management System (SEMS). Issue emergency proclamations and make Federal disaster declaration request. Coordinate requests for Federal assistance; utilize mutual aid regions and operational areas to support and coordinate local and Federal response. Provide training and technical assistance to local agency response organizations. Coordinate nongovernmental organization support for State and local response. Provide and coordinate the flow of information internally and externally to the public.	Provide State financial assistance to affected local governments and other eligible entities for the repair, restoration, and replacement of damaged public facilities and infrastructure. Administer Federal recovery programs to repair public facilities and infrastructure and provide necessary additional funds. Coordinate Federal assistance available for individuals, households, and businesses. Help administer Federal programs for post-disaster mitigation. Administer State-mandated planning, zoning, subdivision, environmental review, and building related requirements.	Participate in national tsunami risk awareness programs. Create and administer public education programs to promote risk awareness, and also fund locally specific efforts.

9

Table 1. Generalized framework for U.S. tsunami disaster policy.—Continued

[Adapted from Topping and others, 2010]

	Mitigation and Preparedness	Response	Recovery	Risk Awareness
Local	Make building-site mitigation improvements to reduce risks to local infrastructure. Prepare and adopt State-mandated city and county general plans, including safety elements, Local Coastal Plans, hazard zones, and building codes. Prepare and adopt FEMA-approved Local Hazard Mitigation Plans.	Have primary responsibility for evacuation and disaster response. Establish priorities for allocation of personnel and resources. Provide information and locally based assessments. Request assistance and mutual aid using tiered relationships. Obtain and disseminate information to the local public. Coordinate laterally with local nongovernmental organizations (NGOs), community-based organizations (CBOs), faith-based organizations (FBOs), medical providers, other local agencies, and private sector. Coordinate vertically with State and Federal agencies/ responders	Primary responsibility for recovery; request State and Federal assistance as necessary. Review and approve permits for repairs and reconstruction in accordance with local plans, zoning and subdivision regulations, the California Environmental Quality Act, the California Coastal Act, and building codes.	Participate in national and State risk awareness programs. Create and administer local tsunami risk awareness programs. Disclose coastal flooding risk (and tsunami information as available) as part of land development and other locally controlled development review.
Private	Buy NFIP and other hazards insurance and business interruption insurance Make building-site mitigation improvements reducing risks to privately owned infrastructure Make building-site mitigation improvements reducing risks to private property.	Coordinate with local agency responders. Provide resources for support of local and regional response efforts. Provide information to emergency responders. Coordinate communication with local businesses and organizations. Coordinate vertically with corporate parent and partner entities and organizations.	Repair and rebuild according to codes and regulations. Businesses and individuals provide resources for recovery via insurance, grants, and reserves. Nongovernmental and philanthropic organizations provide resources for recovery through donations, services and grants.	Mortgage lenders disclose tsunami risk when it is consistent with NFIP mapped coastal flooding areas. Private insurance promotes risk awareness as part of the underwriting process. Create nonprofit organizations to promote two-way risk communication for their particular hazard.

Overarching Policy Consideration

The disaster management policy framework for tsunami hazards and impacts is not as well developed as it is for other hazards and disaster management policy areas in both the State of California and the United States. The lack of experience, risk awareness, and institutionalized planning and implementation practices for tsunami mitigation, preparedness, response, and recovery could amplify impacts and losses from this scenario, even beyond what has been estimated as for coastal government, maritime, business, and tourism sectors and the general public.

This scenario hypothesizes a disaster that can be adequately managed within existing national and State disaster policies. However, there will be gaps—areas where mitigation and preparedness activities were not heeded or fully achieved; areas where the warnings, evacuations, and response activities will not be well executed and coordinated; and areas where the recovery challenges may be significant and take years to resolve. There are also significant gaps in tsunami risk awareness that potentially undermine the effectiveness of the existing disaster policy framework and can negatively influence the response activities and recovery challenges posed by this scenario.

In practice, the U.S. disaster management policies and programs tend to work reasonably well in moderate and localized disasters. However, they are not well equipped to address large-scale or catastrophic events that stretch societal resources. Also, with few modern tsunami experiences in the United States and California, the vast majority of the U.S. disaster policy framework reflects learning from other peril-related events (that is, floods, hurricanes, earthquakes), which, in comparison with this scenario, were more moderate in terms of their spatial extent and likely impacts.

The SAFRR tsunami scenario would affect the entire Pacific coastline of the United States and require a significant multi-State mobilization of response-related resources. The tsunami would begin striking the California coast about 4 to 5 hours after the magnitude 9.1 earthquake occurs offshore of the Alaska Peninsula, and it would inundate California coastal areas unlike any tsunami in recent history. Although State and local agencies would have time to activate emergency operations centers and begin evacuating low-lying coastal areas, harbors and marinas, and reposition boats and ships safely offshore, this would still be a relatively short timeframe to fully evacuate and secure highly populated and congested areas, including public beaches and ports, harbors, and marina facilities. The scenario damage assessment assumes that all the port, business, and governmental entities made timely and correct decisions and actions on saving assets ahead of the scenario tsunami's arrival. Delayed or incorrect decisions/actions, especially with regard to heavily populated areas, marine oil facilities, and tankers and other large ships could significantly increase the potential for escalated losses or cascading impacts.

There is an overarching risk awareness challenge to reach the general public, as well as the special interest sectors, such as the maritime community, and to adequately train and prepare the multiple levels and types of governments needed to mitigate tsunami hazards and prepare to manage the impacts and consequences of this scenario and other potential tsunamis that threaten the State. After all, the SAFRR tsunami scenario is not the "worst case" for a vast part of California's coastline. A major near-field tsunami on the Cascadia Subduction Zone would have a far shorter warning time and could cause far greater devastation, especially in northern California.

The National Tsunami Hazard Mitigation Program (NTHMP), first formed by Congressional action in 1995 and strengthened by the Tsunami Warning and Education Act of 2006, is the major source of Federal support for the Nation's tsunami warning system, the TsunamiReady program that promotes community preparedness for tsunamis, and hazard assessment, mitigation and readiness activities in 28 U.S. coastal States, territories, and commonwealths. Federal funding for the NTHMP is scheduled to end in 2013. Unless the Tsunami Warning and Education Act of 2006 is reauthorized, the foundation of the Nation's and California's tsunami policy framework will be significantly diminished and the future of the TsunamiReady program and State leadership for local tsunami hazard assessment, mitigation and preparedness will be at significant risk.

Priority Policy Issues: Mitigation and Preparedness

Hazard mitigation is a disaster management function ideally preceding and lessening the impacts o, disasters (pre-event mitigation) or helping to reduce repetitive future losses after disasters (post-event mitigation). FEMA defines hazard mitigation as "sustained action taken to reduce or eliminate long-term risk to people and their property from hazards" (FEMA, 2012a). Preparedness is a disaster management function that works to ensure efficient and effective emergency management and response activities during times of crisis. It is "achieved and maintained through a continuous cycle of planning, organizing, training, equipping, exercising, evaluating, and taking corrective action" (FEMA, 2012b). In a sense, mitigation and preparedness are two sides of the same coin. Mitigation works to prevent future losses, whereas preparedness helps to maintain a state of readiness to deal with the expected residual response demands.

Primary Federal legislation fostering tsunami-related mitigation and preparedness includes the National Tsunami Hazard Mitigation Program (NTHMP), the Stafford Act, the Disaster Mitigation Act of 2000 (DMA 2000), and the National Flood Insurance Program (NFIP). National mitigation laws and authorities generally authorize financial support to State and local governments and, in the case of flood insurance, to the private market supporting mitigation actions. In turn, these tend to be mirrored in State laws and programs, such as the California Tsunami Preparedness and Hazard Mitigation Program (TPHMP), and in some cases, local mitigation laws and policies. Additional State legislation and mandates fostering mitigation and preparedness include the safety element requirement of local General Plans, the California Coastal Act (1976), Oil Spill Prevention and Response Act (1990), and permitting requirements of the Bay Conservation and Development Commission (BCDC) for San Francisco Bay. Some key mitigation and preparedness policy issues are (1) lack of a coordinated and sufficiently robust policy framework for tsunami hazard assessment and mitigation planning and (2) disproportionate levels of mitigation and preparedness among California's coastal communities, ports, and harbors.

Need for a Robust Policy Framework for Tsunami Hazard Assessment and Mitigation Planning

California coastal communities and ports and harbors lack a coordinated and sufficiently robust policy framework for tsunami hazard assessment and mitigation planning. California has 20 counties, 100 incorporated and 52 unincorporated cities, 7 major port regions, and more than 100 additional smaller ports, harbors, and marinas that border the Pacific Ocean and San Francisco Bay and are therefore exposed to threats posed by the SAFRR tsunami scenario.

Coastal Communities

Table 2 summarizes the status of tsunami hazard mitigation and planning among Californian's 20 coastal counties and 101 incorporated cities based on a review of their (1) participation in TsunamiReady, (2) participation in NFIP, and (3) demonstrated comment to toward lessening the impact of tsunamis as indicated in Local Hazard Mitigation Plans (LHMP).

The review found that all the coastal counties and incorporated coastal cities participate in the NFIP, whereas, only 35 percent of counties and 16 percent of incorporated cities along California's coastline are designated "TsunamiReady." The number of TsunamiReady communities has been steadily increasing since the 2011 Japanese tsunami. Participation in these two programs provides a rough indication of how risk averse a community is to tsunamis and floods in general.

The LHMPs of coastal counties and incorporated cities were also reviewed to determine if the LHMPs considered tsunami hazards and also whether their Action Plans include mitigation actions specific to tsunami hazard. The results are summarized in three categories: N—the LHMP did not address tsunami hazard; P—the LHMP Action Plan passively addresses the tsunami hazard (broad, general actions that address a multitude of natural hazards including tsunami); and A—the LHMP Action Plan actively and specifically addresses tsunami hazard.

In general, the concern for tsunami hazard appears to increase from the southern to the northern part of the State, which is consistent with the known degree of hazard and experience from historical occurrences. Counties also appear to be more aggressive in addressing tsunami hazard than cities. One-quarter of the county and 44 percent of the incorporated city LHMPs that were reviewed were prepared before 2010 and prior to the Maule, Chile, and Tohoku, Japan, tsunamis. The profiling of tsunami hazard, connectivity with the local safety element and emergency operations plans, and inclusion of tsunami mitigation in action plans has also generally improved in the updated plans.

There is considerable variability in the tsunami hazard mitigation actions planned or undertaken by the majority of coastal counties and incorporated cities. Most are focused on improvements in emergency management with a common action calling for the designation of the community as TsunamiReady. Only a few communities identified significant structural mitigation, such as building a new bridge to facilitate evacuation or improving walk ramps from the beach to higher ground, as priority mitigation actions. This may be partly due to the higher cost of structural mitigations but is most likely due to a priority for life safety, considering the high exposure of existing development, as well as beach populations during summer months.

The review did not evaluate safety elements or local coastal plans (LCPs), which also contain such information. A cursory review of the safety elements for coastal communities found that they contain descriptions of tsunami hazard and history; however, other than general statements regarding the need for new development to avoid areas subject to natural hazards, they do not detail hazard mitigation specifically for tsunami, nor indicate the level of commitment to take action. For most communities, this is likely due to their lack of tsunami experience and also that most safety elements predate recent tsunamis that have caused significant damage in California and elsewhere in the world. Following the 2011 Tohoku Oki tsunami in Japan, the California Coastal Commission added a requirement for the assessment of tsunami hazards for proposed development located in the designated coastal zone and for recertification of LCPs. However, only a few communities have begun the recertification process and only a few plans were available for this review.

Coastal Ports and Harbors

As noted by Wilson and Miller (2013), dozens of California's harbors sustained damage totaling nearly $100 million from the 2010 Chile and 2011 Japan tsunamis even though there wasn't significant inundation of any of California's coastal land from either of these events. Table 3 summarizes the results of a review of the status of tsunami hazard assessment and mitigation planning for the seven major harbor regions identified in the California Oil Spill Prevention and Response Act of 1990—(from south to north) San Diego Port and Harbor; Port of Los Angeles (considers both City of Los Angeles and Los Angeles County); Port of Long Beach; Port Hueneme; San Francisco Bay (includes Port of San Francisco, Port of Oakland, County of San Francisco and Alameda County); San Pablo Bay (includes Port of Richmond and Marin, Sonoma, Napa, Solano, and Contra Costa Counties and the Association of Bay Area Government's multijurisdictional multi-hazard plan); Suisun Bay (includes Solano and Contra

Costa Counties); Humboldt Bay; and Crescent City Harbor (a small harbor with heightened concern for tsunami hazards and shown for comparison).

This review considered whether a port commissioned a special tsunami-hazard analysis or risk assessment that would indicate a heightened awareness and concern about tsunami hazard and risk to operations. To what extent the results of such studies triggered mitigation was not assessed. Outside studies, such as those conducted by a university were noted but did not typically evaluate risk to facilities. The review considered the following factors as proxies to assess the status of tsunami risk awareness, mitigation, and planning for ports and harbors (posed as questions in order of importance):

- Did the LHMP for the county or city where the port is located specifically include tsunami hazard mitigation? Do the mitigation goals/objectives specifically include tsunami hazard? Is there a harbor annex that considers tsunami hazard?
- Is the city or county where the port is located certified as TsunamiReady? Currently none of the major port and harbors are in California are certified as TsunamiReady but some of the cities or counties in which they are located are certified.
- Does the port's harbor safety plan explicitly recognize tsunami threat?
- Does the city or county emergency operations plan explicitly recognize tsunami threat to the port/harbor?

This analysis found that the tsunami hazard has been assessed for all principal ports/harbors except for Port Hueneme, for which the U.S. Navy may have commissioned an evaluation. Overall, perception of the hazard as moderate or serious appears to highest in the northern part of the State and less in the southern part of the State, which is consistent with the known degree of hazard. Exceptions are the Ports of Los Angeles and Long Beach, which have commissioned tsunami hazard and risk studies. Harbor safety plans rarely mention specific natural hazards, including tsunamis, or reference the LHMP and county/city emergency operation plans. Humboldt Bay is an exception. The Humboldt Bay Harbor Safety Plan has a tsunami annex that is also part of the county emergency operations plan. Only Crescent City's LHMP has a port/harbor annex.

Table 2. Status of tsunami hazard assessment and mitigation planning in California coastal counties and incorporated cities.

[LHMP, Local Hazard Mitigation Plan. N, tsunami hazard not addressed in the LHMP Action Plan; P, tsunami hazard passively addressed in the LHMP Action Plan; A, tsunami hazard actively addressed in the LHMP Action Plan. %, percent]

Coastal Jurisdiction	Local Hazard Mitigation Plan (LHMP)	Tsunami in LHMP Action Plan			Designated "TsunamiReady"	Participates in NFIP
		N	P	A		
Counties	100%	25%	30%	45%	35%	100%
Incorporated cities	93%	48%	21%	31%	16%	100%

15

Table 3. Status of tsunami hazard assessment and mitigation planning for California's major ports and harbors.

[Y, yes; N, no; n.a., not applicable; LHMP, Local Hazard Mitigation Plan]

Port/Harbor	San Diego	Los Angeles	Long Beach	Port Heuneme	San Francisco Bay	San Pablo Bay	Suisun Bay	Humboldt Bay	Crescent City Harbor
1. Tsunami risk or hazard assessment?	Y[1]	Y[2]	Y[2]	N	Y[3]	Y[3]	Y[3]	Y[4]	Y
2a. LHMP-harbor annex?	N	N	N	N	N	N	N	Y	Y
2b. LHMP-tsunami goals/objectives?	Y	Y	Y	N	Y	Y[5]	N	Y	Y
2c. LHMP-Tsunami in action plan?	N	Y	Y	N	Y	Y[5]	N	Y	Y
3. Is city/county TsunamiReady™?	Y	Y[6]	N[6]	Y	Y	N	N	N	Y
4. Harbor Safety Plan mentions tsunami?	N	N[6]	N[6]	N	N	N	N	Y[7]	n.a.
5. Emergency plan mentions tsunami?	Y	Y	Y[8]	N	Y	Y	Y	Y	Y

[1] University of Southern California Tsunami Research Center completed new assessment in 2011.

[2] Tsunami hazard/risk assessment done (Uslu and others, 2010; Moffatt and Nichol, 2012).

[3] Special tsunami study done for San Francisco Bay (Borrero and others, 2006).

[4] Tsunami hazard assessment has been done for Humboldt Bay (Uslu and others, 2008).

[5] Marin, Sonoma, and Contra Costa County Local Hazard Mitigation Plans; Association of Bay Area Governments assessment.

[6] Los Angeles County Tsunami Response Plan includes port area.

[7] Humboldt Bay harbor safety plan has extensive annex for tsunami and cross-references to emergency plan.

[8] Harbor safety training includes earthquake safety but not tsunami.

In general, the documents reviewed indicate that the majority of California's coastal communities and ports and harbors more often consider tsunami hazards to be an emergency management issue rather than a land use or development policy issue. There is also a lack of connectivity on tsunami policy issues between various plans in a given community. A more robust and integrated planning framework would help to reinforce knowledge of hazards and the potential impacts, mitigation actions that could be taken to reduce community vulnerability, and improved and more coordinated response efforts across all responsible government agencies during a disaster. The overall policy question raised is what tools, information, and potential legislative actions could help strengthen California's tsunami hazard assessment and mitigation planning policy framework?

How Can Tsunami Hazard Assessment Models and Mapping Be Improved?

CGS, in partnership with the University of Southern California's Tsunami Research Center, has developed a series of tsunami inundation maps for parts of the California coastline to assist emergency managers in developing community evacuation plans (State of California, 2009). The potential tsunami hazard inundation areas shown on these maps are based on the maximum area extent of potential inundation derived from an ensemble of maximum credible events that could occur on near and distant tsunami sources.

The National Research Council's 2011 assessment of the U.S. tsunami program called for more consistent and comprehensive risk mapping and vulnerability nationwide—a national tsunami risk assessment (National Research Council, 2011). Pilot projects funded by NTHMP and FEMA are underway in California to develop more probabilistic approaches to tsunami hazard assessment that account for the likelihood of occurrence and estimates of potential inundation area, flow depth, velocity, and other physical parameters which all could more appropriately support the land-use planning, zoning, and construction related mitigation planning and actions of coastal communities and maritime facilities. Modeling advances made as part of these pilot projects and the SAFRR tsunami scenario can help to better characterize the probabilities of tsunami hazard (for example, at 100-, 500-, 1,000-, and 2,500-year return periods) along California's coast. However, the complexity of such modeling and uncertainties in the model results can present some challenges for public policymaking. To serve as a basis for public policy, advanced tsunami hazard assessment models need to be open and transparent and peer-reviewed or otherwise professionally recognized as "standard-of-practice." Guidelines may also be needed for their testing, evaluation, and use.

How Can Tsunami Hazard Zones Be Defined and Implemented For Community Land-Use Planning, Zoning, and Construction Related Mitigation Planning and Actions?

The California Seismic Hazard Mapping Act explicitly provides for the State Geologist to also map the potential effects of tsunami and seiche when information becomes available from other sources and is deemed appropriate for use by local government. Under the act, an official tsunami hazard zone would trigger tsunami design requirements for proposed construction and existing statutes would also require a site-specific investigation of associated geotechnical hazards and a plan to mitigate identified hazards before a building permit is issued.

An expert advisory committee could provide guidance on the development of the tsunami hazard mapping criteria and other products necessary to support its implementation. The zonation work may also benefit from close consultation with those entities responsible for developing the tsunami resilient codes that are currently under development. Guidelines may also be needed for local agencies responsible for integrating the hazard zones into local land use, zoning, subdivision and development permitting processes as well as LHMPs, LCPs, and the safety elements of local general plans.

Legislative changes may also be needed to ensure better integration of the tsunami hazard zones in State and local planning and development requirements and consistency with any tsunami-resilient building design code provisions that are adopted. Areas subject to policy inconsistencies could include areas where the tsunami hazard zones extend inland beyond the coastal zones and regulatory authorities offered by the California Coastal Act. Communities may want to avoid confusion about tsunami hazard reduction efforts and strive for consistent standards within a jurisdiction's general plan throughout the areal extent of officially designated tsunami hazard zones.

How Can Tsunami Hazard Zones Be Defined and Implemented For Ports and Harbors Related Mitigation Planning and Actions?

CGS is currently developing hazard products tailored for the maritime community that are based on detailed hydrodynamic modeling of harbors to assist in identifying vulnerable port and harbor infrastructure and designating offshore safety zones for evacuation planning and response. More detailed tsunami hazard maps of harbors and channel areas are needed statewide to help identify high-hazard areas (such as areas of high current velocity, turbulence, and eddies) and safer locations for facilities and passageways to reduce the risk of damage to harbor infrastructure and abandoned vessels. Consistent statewide guidelines for maritime tsunami response and recovery are needed and it would be useful to have their development guided by a statewide advisory committee comprised of key State agencies (for example, Cal OES, CGS, CCC, Department of Fish and Wildlife), military (including the U.S. Coast Guard), NOAA, local port harbor authorities, maritime organizations, and key stakeholders. The guidelines could include standards for a more appropriate depth contour for offshore evacuations; hazard thresholds for harbor facilities and vessels; best practices for ship (re)positioning in a tsunami; and recommended protocols for evacuations—when not to evacuate and when to issue an "all clear" following a harbor evacuation. Such information could be distributed to harbor authorities along with guidance or training on their use. Coastal charts and maps could also be revised to be consistent with the new information, and broad communication and dissemination efforts could work to reach various interest groups and stakeholders (for example, military/transport/cruise ships, commercial fishing boats, and recreational boaters, as well as port, wharf/dock, and marina managers).

How Can Tsunami Resilient Building Design Provisions Be Adopted and Implemented?

California's Building Code and the International Building Code (IBC) contain provisions for weather-related flood-resilient design, and all coastal communities participate in the National Flood Insurance Program that requires adherence to specified flood design standards. However, these design standards do not consider the unique characteristics of tsunami-induced flooding. Tsunami resilient design standards are currently under development by the American Society of Civil Engineers (ASCE) Subcommittee on Tsunami Loads and Effects and anticipated for release in 2016. Given this schedule, they would be incorporated into the 2018 edition of the IBC at the earliest. These standards will only address new construction that is initiated once the new building code is in place.

Opportunities may exist to adopt interim provisions once the ASCE standards are released in 2016 or to expedite adoption of the IBC provisions once available. Incentives to encourage local adoption and implementation may also be needed. For example, the Building Code Effectiveness Grading Schedule (BCEGS), which assesses and rates both local building code adoption and enforcement practices, could collaborate in monitoring local implementation and increase community ratings once tsunami resilient building provisions are adopted and enforced.

As coastal engineering codes and standards become more formalized, the State could consider requiring that engineers performing site-specific tsunami inundation and engineering analyses as part of coastal development projects to be a "diplomate" with Coastal Engineering certification from the ASCE Academy of Coastal, Ocean, Port, and Navigation Engineers (COPNE) (American Society of Civil Engineers, 2013). The State might also consider developing its own certification for civil engineers specializing in coastal engineering.

The Tsunami Scenario Would Have Severe Impacts

The tsunami scenario would severely impact communities and ports and harbors that have made sustained tsunami mitigation and preparedness efforts, as well as those that have not. This could result in varying levels of impacts, potentially including significant life losses and demands for response and recovery resources. Most of California's coastal neighborhoods, businesses and industries, and infrastructure have not been built to withstand tsunami forces. Under such conditions, life safety is of paramount importance, which puts mitigation and preparedness planning at the forefront of risk reduction strategies. But, as the planning analyses have shown, tsunami hazard awareness, mitigation and preparedness planning, and actions vary considerably across California's communities and ports and harbors.

Funding for predisaster mitigation, under the Stafford Act and Disaster Mitigation Act is infinitesimally small relative to the nationwide need and it has historically tended to reward good mitigation performance through additional funding (Topping and others, 2010). And, the TsunamiReady program, as a voluntary program, is more apt to attract better mitigation performers seeking this designation. And, thus in the SAFRR tsunami scenario or another major tsunami affecting the West Coast, there will likely be areas with significant damage and potential life loss, whereas other areas will emerge relatively unscathed.

There are both funding and engagement challenges in getting the most vulnerable and unprepared coastal communities and ports and harbors to voluntarily undertake mitigation and preparedness actions ahead of a tsunami disaster. More coastal communities need to be encouraged to participate in the TsunamiReady program. There also needs to be enhanced coordination and information sharing among coastal communities on tsunami mitigation and preparedness plans and actions, which might be a State-led program activity. This includes promoting better sharing of best practices and developing multi-jurisdictional evacuation and response plans.

The community planning analysis also found that coastal county and city participants in the TsunamiReady program did not meet the program guidelines equally effectively. A review of standards for program designation and development of a process for ongoing maintenance of the TsunamiReady designation may also be useful in ensuring that TsunamiReady designated communities are indeed ready for the impacts of a future tsunami.

Coastal communities and regional government associations might also need to be more strongly encouraged to work more collaboratively on tsunami hazard mitigation and preparedness planning. Neighboring communities could also be encouraged to integrate their local hazard mitigation plans into a multi-jurisdictional plan that would help qualify as an enhanced plan and be eligible for the associated disaster recovery assistance benefits under the Stafford Act and the Disaster Mitigation Act. The State Hazard Mitigation Plan could also be strengthened to provide more direction to coastal communities by addressing broad regional issues and helping to shape tsunami hazard mitigation strategies for local communities to follow. Alternative sources of funding for advance planning and mitigation are also needed, especially if Federal or State support for the NTHMP ends.

Additional emphasis needs to be placed on ensuring that the State's many ports, harbors, and maritime facilities also undertake mitigation and preparedness planning and actions. Currently, there is limited data available on marina damage and tsunami loss modeling for marinas is just in its infancy. As described in Wilson and Miller (2013), the State, through the NTHMP, has been working to enhance the information and resources available for the maritime community on tsunami preparedness and response planning and preparedness planning is underway at some of the State's largest ports. Harbor authorities could be further encouraged to prepare tsunami preparedness, response, and recovery plans for their facilities. State guidelines for maritime tsunami response and recovery, along with a robust dissemination and training program, also could be developed.

Priority Policy Issues: Response

For tsunamis, emergency response begins when a potential tsunami threat is identified and the threat analysis and notification protocols are initiated. These functions are Federally led by NOAA's national tsunami warning centers which issue Alert Bulletins designating a tsunami WATCH, ADVISORY or WARNING. There are standardized templates for the series of alert bulletins that also contain information regarding first wave arrival times and projected wave amplitudes for specified locations. The alert bulletins are disseminated using many redundant communication paths, including the NOAA Weather Wire Service, NOAA Weather Radio (NWR), Emergency Managers Weather Information Network (EMWIN), email/cell phone text messaging, Emergency Alert System (EAS), U.S. Coast Guard and U.S. Navy, and the Integrated Public Alert and Warning System (IPAWS).

The California State Warning Center (CSWC) is the designated Warning Point agency authorized to transmit the national tsunami alert bulletins statewide. The CSWC forwards information it receives to Cal OES and county emergency management offices. It does not, however, independently designate alert levels; only the national tsunami warning center can designate the alert level. All information from the West Coast and Alaska Tsunami Warning Center (WCATWC) is passed directly to the counties by redundant methods as well. The public and media get this information almost simultaneously through the variety of communications systems.

Once a credible tsunami threat is confirmed, Cal OES regional and State operation centers initiate a series of conference call briefings for California's coastal counties and State agencies. Under California's Standard Emergency Management System (SEMS), each county in California is an operational area (OA) and responsible for notifying and coordinating with their local jurisdictions (cities and special districts) and unincorporated areas through multiple, redundant means.

Local jurisdictions are responsible for ordering evacuations within their geographic limits; counties are the "local authority" for unincorporated county areas. Local jurisdictions and port authorities, where they exist, generally share civil authority over evacuations of low-lying coastal areas. Port authorities, harbor masters, and the U.S. Coast Guard are responsible for offshore evacuation and directing the movement of boats and ships out of harbors to deep waters. Depending on the alert level, and local vulnerability, past experience, and plans, initial decisions may range from waiting for further information, initiating a phased evacuation, or ordering a total evacuation. Most counties and local jurisdictions in California have developed local methods for disseminating emergency messages, including the Emergency Alert System (EAS), residential telephone emergency notification system (TENS; similar to Reverse 911), sirens, local radio communications, media announcements, and others. As noted by Brosnan and others (written commun., 2013), some of California's fishing communities have also developed emergency communication systems and protocols.

Some key response policy issues are (1) challenges with existing warning dissemination and evacuation information and protocols and localized disruptions of communications systems; (2) lack of experience and gaps in policy and guidelines for handling a major tsunami evacuation, sheltering, and extended security of evacuated areas; and (3) significant demands on different levels of government and the need for cooperation at each tier and within every organization involved in the response.

Onshore/Offshore Evacuations and Emergency Response Will Be Challenged by Existing Warning/Evacuation Protocols and Disruptions To Communications

The coordination and effectiveness of both onshore and offshore evacuations and emergency response activities will be challenged by existing tsunami warning dissemination and evacuation information and protocols and localized disruptions to communications systems. In the SAFRR tsunami, a large earthquake occurs offshore of the Alaska Peninsula, at 10:50 Pacific Daylight Time (PDT) on Thursday, March 27, 2014. NOAA issues the first tsunami alert bulletin within 3 minutes of the earthquake's occurrence. The bulletin activates a WARNING for the coastal areas of British Columbia and Alaska and a WATCH for the coastal areas of Washington, Oregon, and California. Initial arrival times are estimated to range from 16:02 PDT at Crescent City, California (a little more than 5 hours) to 17:38 PDT at La Jolla, California (about 6½ hours). The Emergency Alert System is also activated at this time and begins relaying the notifications to emergency management systems and personnel, television, and radio stations.

Local emergency managers are immediately faced with a dilemma—wait for the next alert bulletin which will confirm the tsunami and better estimate the arrival time or begin evacuations and response activities immediately to ensure that evacuations and infrastructure protection are completed in a timely and safe manner? The managers at the seven major ports and more than 100 smaller marinas and harbors also face similar evacuation decisions as soon as they hear the news. This will likely be the first tsunami experience for much of the maritime community, which also may not have emergency plans or may have limited experience with offshore evacuations. Few California residents, especially in the San Francisco Bay area and Southern California, have much experience with tsunamis or mass evacuations.

In the SAFRR tsunami scenario, the first official notification that puts California into the WARNING stage and offers the first information about estimated wave heights and duration comes at 12:05 PDT. It forecasts the tsunami reaching Crescent City at 15:58 PDT (less than 4 hours), San Francisco at 16:55 PDT (less than 5 hours), San Pedro at 17:27 PDT, and La Jolla at 17:38 PDT (less than 5½ hours). The maximum tsunami heights are forecast to reach 10.1 feet (+/- 3.0 feet) in Crescent City, 5.0 feet (+/- 1.5 feet) in San Francisco, 3.7 feet (+/- 1.1 feet) in San Pedro, and 8.4 feet (+/-2.5 feet) in La Jolla. The durations are forecast to range from 18 to 48 hours.

Reliable and redundant communications systems will be crucial to evacuation decision makers and emergency responders, as well as the evacuees (both onshore and offshore). Responders will need to communicate with each other to manage both onshore and offshore evacuations and response activities, and individuals and vessel operators will need to receive updates of the tsunami warnings/alerts and notifications of when it is safe to return.

The public's primary sources of information during a disaster are the media and landline phones and cellular networks. The phone and cellular communication networks may be overwhelmed during the initial evacuation period and more remote and significantly impacted coastal areas, particularly in Northern California, are likely to experience system disruptions once the tsunami begins. What will happen when elements of the communication network are broken or diminished in capacity? What will be the "workarounds" necessary for the coordination to take place? What if the disruptions continue for long periods of time, such as weeks or months?

What Alert Dissemination Protocols and Communication System Improvements are Needed to Ensure Safe and Timely Evacuations?

In this scenario and for other near-source tsunamis, waiting for WARNING alert leaves very little time to complete safe and timely evacuations. Since the 2011 Japan tsunami, the national tsunami warning centers have been improving and standardizing how warnings are disseminated to State and local agencies in order to address some of the warning confusion, problems with Web access, and other issues reported at the time. The SAFRR tsunami scenario provides a useful source of information to test revised protocols and see what improvements could be made to alert dissemination protocols.

In recent tsunamis, alert notifications have also triggered inappropriate reactions by parts of the public, especially those who are unfamiliar with the tsunami hazard and what the alert levels mean. Additional explanations of how to respond to NOAA-issued Tsunami Alerts (WATCH, WARNING, and ADVISORY) could also be part of emergency management education and coordination with the media.

Once the tsunami has subsided, local response agencies are responsible for issuing "all clear" messages and allowing reentry into evacuated areas. Similarly, port authorities, harbor masters, and the U.S. Coast Guard will be determining when to allow vessel operators to return to shore. These decisions are often made with little to no scientific information. The tsunami warning centers could be encouraged to develop guidelines and protocols for providing hazard updates/information to help local response agencies decide when to issue the "all clear."

On an annual basis, Cal OES collaborates with the NOAA Weather Forecast Office in Eureka and the Redwood Coast Tsunami Work Group to conduct a multicounty test of the EAS. Considerable planning goes into this "live-code" warning communications test, and such tests need to be continued and expanded to other parts of the California coast. Development and full implementation of the FEMA-Federal Communications Commission wireless-carrier partnership for the Commercial Mobile Alert System (CMAS), Next Gen 911, Reverse 911 and regional broadband public safety networks in California needs to be continued. These systems need to develop the capability to focus messages to specific regions to prevent unnecessary disruption in unaffected areas.

Experience in Japan demonstrated the potential effectiveness of broadcasting evacuation warnings through cellular networks to the general public using mobile phone applications. Implementation in the United States and California would require formal agreements between government agencies that issue warnings and cellular network providers, and the development of mobile phone applications for the general public to use to receive tsunami evacuation warnings.

Lack of Experience in Dealing With the Complexity of a Major Tsunami Evacuation, Sheltering, and Extended Security of Evacuated Areas

There is a lack of experience among California's State and local emergency responders, port and government managers as well as gaps in policy and guidelines for dealing with the complexity of a major tsunami evacuation, sheltering, and extended security of evacuated areas. Local jurisdictions are responsible for developing tsunami evacuation and response plans but, as the community planning analysis showed, there are varying levels of tsunami hazard awareness and preparedness included in local plans and policy. The short fuse nature of this evacuation scenario is going to present some crucial challenges for evacuation management, especially for public venues, critical facilities, schools, hospitals, and dependent-care facilities near the coast and beaches.

Many local emergency managers are likely to rely on the maximum tsunami hazard zones published on California's tsunami inundation maps, because the likely extent of the tsunami will not be known until it arrives. What also will not be known until later is that the inundation area for the SAFRR scenario tsunami directly impacts far fewer residents (91,956) and business employees (81,277) than those located in the State's tsunami inundation maps (267,347 residents and 168,565 employees). Being too quick or overly conservative in determining which areas to evacuate can be costly for coastal businesses, public safety, and public confidence, but being too late or limiting the evacuation area can be catastrophic.

There are also some "hot spots" where the concentrations of residents and employees at risk of inundation are quite high. These include Huntington Beach, Newport Beach, Los Angeles, and Long Beach in southern California; Oakland, Alameda, Emeryville, and Belvedere in the San Francisco Bay area; and Crescent City in northern California. Also, as noted by Wood and others (2013), some of these areas are further challenged by access limitations, with few roads, bridges, or pedestrian pathways off island or out of low-lying areas.

The ports planning analysis showed that there are also varying levels of tsunami hazard awareness and preparedness at California's major ports; smaller ports and harbors may have done little planning because none is currently required. Port authorities, harbormasters, the U.S. Coast Guard and others involved in evacuation decision making must consider safety and protection of populations and assets on the water as well as on land. On land, employees working at port terminals and other facilities must be notified and evacuated. In the water, decisions must be made about vessels currently in the port and harbor areas as well as those attempting to enter.

Vessel-related decisions will likely involve differing recommendations based on vessel size and weather and ocean/tide conditions —which vessels to evacuate offshore and how much time is available and needed by each vessel to do so? Small craft marinas are especially vulnerable to the high currents associated with tsunamis, and offshore evacuations of recreational vessels are rarely feasible and not encouraged by State emergency managers. Also, unlike onshore evacuees, offshore evacuation decision makers and the vessel operators must carefully consider prolonged safety issues—having enough food, water, and fuel for extended periods (an estimated 2 to 4 days for this tsunami scenario) and whether their vessels can get to more distant harbors if their home port is destroyed. Many operators may not get the message in time, or have time to get a crew aboard to allow the vessel to safely depart before the tsunami's arrival. As described in Brosnan and others (written commun., 2013), decisions will also need to be made about whether it is appropriate to leave personnel onboard vessels during the tsunami event or evacuate them back to shore.

After coastal areas and ports have been evacuated, local responders will also have to manage security and re-entry. Traffic checkpoints will need to be established at the edge of the evacuation zones to direct and restrict traffic from coming back into dangerous areas. Additional traffic control points may also need to be established at strategic locations further inland to reduce traffic flow toward the coast. Emergency equipment will need to be staged outside the inundation area. Maritime security will similarly need to be provided and likely to involve waterway patrols. Loose or unauthorized large vessels moving in a closed port could cause significant damage. Some people will inevitably be unable to make it out in time before local responders begin to leave the danger zones before the tsunami's arrival. Air rescues are likely to be carried out by the U.S. Coast Guard and other qualified agencies and personnel. Given the widespread and complex of impacts along the coast and ports, there will be significant staffing requirements to secure the vast evacuation perimeter up and down the State. This will all require multiagency coordination. Often, cooperating agencies develop a Multiagency Coordination System (MACS) to better define how they will work together and to work together more efficiently; however, multiagency coordination can take place without established protocols.

Any people who do not evacuate will need to be instructed to seek opportunities for "vertical" evacuation and resist the urge to evacuate during the tsunami inundation. Typically, the first tsunami wave is not the highest, and tidal variations could increase the risk of the later waves. Local responders will also be instructed to remain outside the danger zones until an "all clear" for responders is issued, but they too will be pressured to help before the tsunami recedes.

The extended duration of this tsunami scenario will mean that many evacuees will need overnight shelter and, for the most heavily impacted communities, evacuations may turn into protracted displacements. It is estimated that 8,489 people will require shelter for the SAFRR tsunami scenario. However, relying on the State's tsunami inundation maps, emergency managers would be collectively responding to provide shelter for a much larger number of displaced people than may be necessary. In addition to shelters, reception, refuge, feeding and staging areas will be needed. As Wood and others (2013) reveal, there will also be special needs issues with impacted populations including tourists, non-English speakers, very old or very young people, and people from group quarters and dependent care facilities, including schools, colleges and jails.

In this scenario, the WARNING is cancelled at 12 to 14 hours after the earthquake's occurrence; however, in and along waterfront areas, strong tsunami currents will likely continue. Once they are given the "all clear," local responders begin "windshield surveys" and initial safety assessments to determine search and rescue and other response needs and plan for an orderly reentry. Areas that were not inundated will likely be given the "all clear" quickly, whereas a phased or facilitated reentry may be needed where damage or continuing hazards exist.

According to Porter and others (2013), there will be at least two days in which operations at major ports will be halted in the SAFRR scenario. The first day will consist of safely shutting down and securing operations, deploying tug boats, removing vessels where possible, and generally preparing for the tsunami arrival and evacuation of personnel. The second day would be focused on inspections of facilities prior to restoring operations. All loading and unloading equipment will be disengaged to prevent damage from tsunami waves and currents, as well as any sudden power losses.

As Plumlee and others (2013) and Brosnan and others (written commun., 2013) describe, debris fields, fires, fuel leaks, hazardous material spills, and damaged and unsafe structures all may exist in flooded coastal and port areas. Sunk or beached vessels may affect port and harbor navigation. Debris clearance, contamination clean up, and utility restoration could take days to weeks to complete, especially if the damages are significant. Helping displaced residents and vessel operators to return will also require coordination. There may be public health issues to consider as contaminated water could impact soils and structures inundated by flooding. For some areas, sheltering of displaced populations may also continue for some time.

What Additional Plans, Policies, and Guidelines Are Needed to Deal With the Complexity of Both Onshore and Offshore Tsunami Evacuation, Sheltering, and the Extended Security of Evacuated Areas?

For most coastal communities, the SAFRR scenario inundations will not extend as far inland as the maximum inundation line shown on the State's tsunami inundation maps. The State TPHMP is currently developing tsunami evacuation "playbooks" that will provide more detailed models of potential inundation areas for a number of different tsunami scenarios. Playbook maps will show expected areas of flooding for tsunamis of various wave heights, such as one, two, three and four meters above the Mean High Water (high tide) line. Other scenarios in the playbooks will provide modeled inundation lines for a magnitude 9.2 eastern Aleutians tsunami; worst-case tsunami scenarios for specific local sources, such as submarine faults and landslides, that might arrive on shore within 10 minutes; and a magnitude 9+ Cascadia scenario that will arrive on shore within about 10 minutes along the northern California coast and within 2 hours along the rest of the California coast. According to Wilson and Miller (2013), a formula that incorporates forecasted tsunami amplitudes (wave heights), tidal conditions, storm activity, and site-specific tsunami run-up potential into a "maximum predicted tsunami run-up height" is being developed to determine which evacuation scenario is most appropriate and conservative to use. These products are expected to be available by the end of 2013. They are intended to assist coastal emergency managers in preparing local evacuation response plans that are more tsunami source specific.

Only a few of California's ports, harbors, and marinas, have conducted detailed studies of potential tsunami in-harbor hazards and risks to facilities. To help address the information gap, the State TPHMP is also developing a set a products for maritime communities: (1) detailed maps identifying in-harbor tsunami hazards, such as potential harbor areas with strong currents and eddies, peak amplitude surges, large tidal fluctuations; (2) offshore safety zones where ships can evacuate to and safely gather during a tsunami; and (3) planning guidelines for evacuations, response and recovery. The maritime mapping and guidelines are expected to be completed by 2015.

The SAFRR tsunami scenario will ultimately serve as a useful tool for emergency management training and exercises and for testing and improving existing policies and plans. It provides important justification of the need for both the community playbooks and maritime planning products and the need for robust dissemination and training efforts associated with their release. More coordination in tsunami preparedness and response planning could be encouraged among adjacent coastal communities. Communities could also be encouraged to share evacuation plans and maps and collaborate on key public education and training messages. The State TPHMP and regional associations of governments along the coast could play a critical in helping promote and facilitate multi-community collaboration.

The scenario also raises some additional policy issues that might be considered in existing or future national and State tsunami program efforts. How to provide more time-based guidance on evacuations in a variety of potential inundation areas and harbor areas? How to manage multimodal evacuations (for example, on foot, by boat, by private car or truck, and using public transportation), as well as the suitability of vertical evacuations? Many of the California's coastal areas, particularly ports, islands and peninsulas, such as in Newport Beach, have limited egress options. Adding pedestrian bridges or vertical evacuation sites could provide significant life safety benefits. Another issue is how to effectively maintain security during a protracted evacuation of both communities and port areas?

Given the broad geographic nature of the SAFRR tsunami scenario, it will be important to provide clear and consistent information to the media and public throughout the response period and to also tailor messaging as needed to different communities, regions, and response issues. The SAFRR scenario provides a good opportunity to test State, local, and Federal communications plans and coordinate with the media on appropriate public-safety messaging during various stages of the tsunami response—notification, evacuation areas and routes, sheltering, reentry and other real-time updates on developments as they occur.

Response Effectiveness Will Depend on Cooperation and Coordination at All Levels of Government

The widespread nature of this large-scale West Coast tsunami scenario would place significant demands on different levels of government. Response effectiveness will depend on cooperation and coordination of operations at each tier and within every organization in the system. For the tsunami scenario, local, State, and Federal level emergency and disaster proclamations are likely to be made quickly. The U.S. response framework will be initiated as defined at the Federal level by the National Incident Management System (NIMS) and National Response Framework (NRF) and carried forward by State, county, and local agencies. FEMA will likely activate its National Operations Coordination Center and its Regional Operations Centers. State emergency management agencies, including Cal OES, will activate their State operations centers as well as any regional operations commands. Local emergency managers will activate their emergency operations centers and depending on the need may request mutual aid or State assistance using established processes.

The U.S. framework is predicated on the principles of (FEMA, 2013):

· "Engaged partnership" both vertically and horizontally among various agencies, both public and private.
· "Tiered response" to recognize local primacy for response and to overlap and establish lines of authority and communication along the vertical continuum from the local up to the Federal level.
· "Scalable, flexible, and adaptable response" so that roles and relationships are clearly outlined and remain the same in any scale of disaster, even though the amount of resources may vary according to the needs of the event.
· "Unity of effort/unity of command" to avoid duplication in effort, confusion, and overlapping/overstepping actions.
· "Readiness to act," train, and prepare so that the emergency responders understand the system at their own level and are prepared to coordinate through the chain of coordination envisioned in the "Engaged Partnership."

A fundamental assumption embedded in the response framework is that, in fact, the system structure can be effectively scaled up to a disaster of any size, and coordination, information flow, and communication are the fundamental building blocks of this multi-governmental and multi-organizational style of response. Although well proven in more limited emergency events, there have been few tests of the system in dealing with a widespread event, like the SAFRR tsunami scenario. The system will only be as strong as its weakest link. FEMA and Cal OES and other West Coast State emergency management agencies, as well as the multitude of local and maritime emergency responders, have limited experience with tsunamis, and most tsunami in the recent past have come from distant sources allowing some lead time for evacuations and preparations. FEMA and California counties are working on an Earthquake and Tsunami Response Plan for the West Coast, focusing on the consequences of a Cascadia Subduction Zone earthquake and tsunami (see Redwood Coast Tsunami Work Group Facebook page, *accessed August 23, 2013* at *https://www.facebook.com/RCTWG?filter=3*).

A second key element is the high level of responsibility delegated to the local agencies to manage the disaster, in effect the "bottom up" approach that the system is built on. This means that response effectiveness depends first and foremost on the capacity and capability of the local actors on the scene. Will local governments and port and harbor facilities have functional capacity to effectively activate and operate the local emergency response, communication, and coordination protocols? Will there be sufficient numbers of knowledgeable personnel to handle emergency operations functions through the tsunami's duration? How will State and Federal actors determine when and how to respond in a situation where there is wide unevenness in the capacity and capabilities of various local actors? When and how will county and State agencies initiate their assessments of unmet needs and identify outside resources through mutual aid, State resources and requests for Federal assistance? How will resources (equipment, supplies, personnel—all potentially scarce or not matched to need geographically) be allocated among multiple and competing needs? Will State and Federal response structures be stretched by the breadth and duration of the event that their effectiveness is compromised?

How will the need to reach far outside the impacted areas to mobilize and obtain needed resources affect the timing and delivery of support?

Experience has shown that in some disasters, the responders defined in an emergency response plan are not always the ones who take on key roles and responsibilities. In these instances, ad hoc organizational structures were created by local leadership because for any number of reasons that proves to be the most effective way to proceed. How will the United States' and California's premise of unity of command be affected when people less trained are substituted into the response roles and systems? How will ad hoc structures be tethered to the command structure and tiered response system? What are effective ways of utilizing ad hoc community or private structures to take advantage of the capacities they provide?

Priority Policy Issues: Recovery

Once the tsunami subsides, and threats to life-safety and property are stabilized, the recovery process along California's coast will begin. Because this scenario will likely trigger a Presidential disaster declaration, Federal assistance for individuals and families, government agencies, tribal organizations, and private nonprofit organizations will be available under the Stafford Act. The National Disaster Recovery Framework (FEMA, 2011) would also begin to guide Federal agency coordination and assistance, and Cal OES's Recovery Branch would deploy, along with FEMA and other Federal personnel, to affected coastal areas. Early recovery activities would include damage assessment, restoration of utilities and community services, and addressing short-term housing and business needs. Long-term repairs, rebuilding and other recovery activities would then likely continue for many months and even years, especially in the most heavily impacted coastal areas.

This section presents two key policy issues: (1) post-disaster recovery challenges for the hardest hit coastal communities, ports and harbors, and parts of the State's fishing and agriculture sectors and (2) challenges of rebuilding more resiliently for a historically infrequent hazard, like tsunami.

Unprecedented Recovery Challenges for Hardest Hit Coastal Communities, Ports and Harbors, and Fishing and Agriculture Sectors

The tsunami scenario would generate unprecedented recovery challenges for the hardest hit coastal communities, ports and harbors, and parts of the State's fishing and agriculture sectors. The tsunami scenario would affect approximately 1,840 Census blocks statewide and produce an estimated $1.8 billion in building and content damage (roughly 2.2 percent of building value and 18 percent of content value in these census blocks). Areas where tsunami building damage would be concentrated could require long-term access limitations, which, unless well secured, could lead to looting and extensive blight. There would also be significant needs for both short-term and long-term housing and business facilities. Any long-term population and business relocations could negatively affect community recovery. In addition to buildings, coastal roads, bridges, and railroads will also sustain damage. Building and infrastructure damage clusters would likely exist in pockets along the entire California coast and around San Francisco Bay.

According to Porter and others (2013), damage is expected to be modest in most of California's major ports, especially if large vessels were successfully evacuated. Two of Southern California's major ports—the Ports of Los Angeles and Long Beach—are expected to sustain direct damages amounting to $113 million, mainly to imported vehicles, containers, and some waterfront facilities. Land-based commerce for most major ports would likely return to service within one or two days following the tsunami scenario with a few facility exceptions where tsunami-related flooding damages buildings and other maritime facilities. Maritime transportation could take longer to restore due to debris and sedimentation issues in the navigation channels or a lengthy cleanup caused by an oil spill into port waters. Rose and others (2013) estimate that direct economic impacts to southern California and the rest of California caused by a 2-day shutdown at major ports as well as facility downtime and cargo losses, could amount to $1.2 billion.

Other harbors and marinas across the State would likely sustain damage estimated at about $600 million. According to Porter and others (2013), more than 5,600 smaller watercraft would sink (about 1 in 7), 7,900 smaller watercraft would be damaged but repairable (about 1 in 5), 140 docks would be destroyed (1 in 6), and 5,350 docks would be damaged but repairable (about half). Small craft that are damaged and become free floating will be a debris issue during and after the tsunami. Some of these may sink in the center of the navigation channels and may pose a navigation issue for other vessels until they are removed.

For those ports, harbors, and marinas that have significant sediment deposition and damage, the permitting process for sediment removal, as well as the complexities of the removal and reconstruction processes, could prolong their recovery for a year or more. Major issues include whether the debris contains contaminants and whether the sediment can be disposed in the ocean or has to be transported to landfills. An underwater inspection may be required before port channels can be reopened. There could be potentially lengthy Federal and State agency approvals, followed by logistical and coordination issues.

As Brosnan and others (written commun., 2013) describe, the fishing industry statewide is also vulnerable to damage to boats and infrastructure (for example, docks, processing plants) from tsunami waves, currents, and debris and other factors. Damage to harbors and onshore fishing facilities and protracted boat repairs could also result in losses and extended impacts to the fishing industry.

According to Ratliff and Wein (2013), approximately 9,600 acres of agricultural land lies in the scenario inundation zone; this is a very small part of the approximately 25 million acres of agricultural land in the State. Non-crop uses such as pastureland make up the majority of inundated agriculture, at 57 percent of the total. Alfalfa farming occupies 42 percent of inundated agricultural land, and truck-transported crops and field crops represent 0.5 percent and 0.4 percent, respectively, of inundated agricultural land. Humboldt County has the highest percentage of inundated agricultural land; San Luis Obispo, Mendocino, and Sonoma Counties also have relatively high percentages. Salinization, debris deposition, soil scour, and contamination all present long-term issues that would need to be carefully and quickly dealt with in order to minimize downtime for affected farms. Most of the exposed agricultural acres lie in the poorer northern counties of the State, and recovery costs could be extensive, slowing recovery and further impacting farming businesses and employees in these counties.

What Recovery Financing Resources and Gaps Are Likely for the Tsunami Scenario?

In California, more than 10,000 people would likely register for FEMA Individual Assistance which would provide funds for emergency housing, housing repairs, and contents replacement. There would likely be significant recovery financing challenges for all impacted residential properties and tenants that do not have National Flood Insurance Program (NFIP) or other insurance coverage. Higher valued residential properties (for example, condominiums, apartment complexes, properties owned by real estate investment trusts) tend to have excess-NFIP insurance coverage. Ensuring that people living in the mapped tsunami inundation zones also have flood insurance could help close the residential recovery funding gaps.

Similarly, impacted small commercial and industrial business owners and property owners, including fisherman, private marina owners, and fishing and harbor facility owners, without NFIP or other insurance coverage would also face recovery financing challenges and could be encouraged to carry NFIP or other commercial flood insurance. Small Business Administration (SBA) post-disaster loans would be a critical recovery resource for impacted small businesses and apartment owners, but these sectors would be challenged to accept additional debt burdens. Private insurance is more likely to be carried by medium and large commercial and industrial businesses and would provide resources for structural and contents related losses related to flooding (that is, excess NFIP). Many businesses in the hardest hit areas would be challenged to sustain themselves over a prolonged recovery period of time with limited resources (both funds and supplies) and displaced markets. As described by Wein and others (2013), long-term business and economic interruptions are not expected to be significant, but these losses would largely be unfunded.

FEMA Public Assistance (PA) is designed to cover emergency response costs and repair costs for public facilities and infrastructure, including publicly owned port, marina, and harbor facilities. Thousands of claims would be likely in California alone from qualifying State and local governments, nonprofits, and utility providers. However, given that the tsunami scenario would affect the entire West Coast of the United States, it is important to consider that the PA program would simultaneously be addressing losses in Alaska and other West Coast States, which could delay the distribution of these funds by a year or two into the recovery.

Also, the Public Assistance program is essentially a reimbursement-based program, and State and local government agencies and other qualifying entities would need to front-end the costs until reimbursements are made. They also would need to provide the required 25 percent match of the Stafford Act programs. Although reimbursement is the preferred method for funding Public Assistance costs, regulations give FEMA the authority to provide advances for immediate needs. Similarly, FEMA has the regulatory ability to waive the local share and provide 100 percent funding for a limited period of time, usually for a designated emergency period.

The tsunami scenario could also result in a fiscal crisis for local governments and special districts struggling to meet the response and recovery needs of such a scenario, while simultaneously facing significant sales and property tax revenue reductions due. This would be especially true in coastal communities that depend heavily on tourism, agricultural, and maritime activities or face significant housing losses or declining home values in the aftermath of the tsunami scenario. The impacts could have cascading effects, as localities and special districts turn to county and State levels for financial assistance. Local governments and utility providers do typically carry some levels of private insurance, although the coverage may not be sufficient.

Private insurance would also provide some resources to the medium and large ports that carry it. However, recovery financing would likely be an issue for those that are uninsured as well as smaller ports, harbors, marinas, and other maritime and fishing businesses that are unlikely to be insured. Agricultural business recovery would also face long-term term financial challenges in restoring losses caused by floodwaters, addressing soil pollution and hazard materials issues, and any longer-term delays in crop restoration and maturity. Post-disaster agricultural assistance programs would be critical to this sector's recovery, but these often come in the form of loans requiring repayment and having rather stringent rules.

There would likely be significant pressure placed on Congress to pass supplemental disaster funding legislation to collectively address the multi-State and Federal recovery needs posed by both the Alaska Peninsula earthquake and tsunami. Supplemental disaster funding approved by Congress after recent disasters, such as Hurricanes Sandy and Katrina, funded a multitude of needs, including housing repair programs, additional funding for community facilities and infrastructure restoration, private property buyouts in hazardous areas, and economic restoration and development projects. However, given current Federal fiscal challenges, such political action may be difficult in future disasters, and California could also be competing with Oregon, Washington, and Alaska for allocations. States would need to cooperate in advocating for and allocating any resulting funds.

What Additional Plans, Policies, and Guidelines Assist the Recovery of California's Coastal Communities and Ports and Harbors Following a Major Tsunami?

California's State and local emergency management agencies and other agencies normally involved in environmental review, land use, development, and construction have limited experience dealing with a large-scale, statewide recovery and rebuilding effort like the one posed by the SAFRR tsunami scenario. The National Disaster Recovery Framework (NDRF) provides guidance on how Federal agencies will coordinate to support key recovery support functions of: community planning and capacity building, economics, health and social services, housing, infrastructure systems, and natural and cultural resources (FEMA, 2011). It also calls for the appointment of Federal and State disaster recovery coordinators as well as local disaster recovery managers (LDRM) with post-disaster responsibilities to (1) lead in the creation of recovery organizations and initiatives and to coordinate their activities and (2) to work with State and Federal recovery partners in damage and impact assessments, prioritizing recovery issues and needs, identifying recovery funding sources, measuring recovery progress, and ensuring effective and consistent communication with stakeholders and the public (FEMA, 2011).

A statewide or regional coordinating, or advising, body may be needed to help craft policy and coordinate financing and long-term recovery technical assistance to impacted coastal communities, businesses, and individuals. The State currently has some legal mechanisms in place (for example, State redevelopment legislation, geologic hazard abatement districts, and the Disaster Recovery and Reconstruction Act) that could aid in these kinds of efforts. Regional associations of governments could also provide leadership to coastal counties, cities, special districts, and unincorporated areas to collaborate and coordinate in advance recovery planning, especially on issues of resource sharing and regional concern. Such planning might use the SAFRR scenario or consider the likely impacts, particularly on regionally shared transportation, water, power and other essential facilities and lifelines, for larger and/or more localized tsunamis that are expected to impact the region. In turn, coastal cities, counties, and special districts (including school, water, and port and harbor districts) could be encouraged to prepare operational recovery plans utilizing findings from the tsunami scenarios. State and local governments may need to take special efforts to involve the maritime and coastal agricultural communities in understanding their potential losses and planning for post-tsunami recovery.

Plans, policies and guidelines that are used in normal times to guide land use, development, and construction will inevitably need modifications to deal with the time-compressed, decision environment of post-disaster recovery (Olshansky and others, 2012). As reported by Plumlee and others (2013), port dredging and disposal and debris removal, both onshore and offshore, are crucial post-disaster problems with potentially complex regulatory and permitting processes. Streamlining these post-disaster processes while also ensuring environmental protection could substantially benefit local community recovery. Policies and programs may also need to be developed to address the removal of contaminated top soil, desalinization of soils, and the detoxification of concrete and other affected building materials. Although regulatory exemptions exist for disaster repair projects under the National Environmental Policy Act and the California Environmental Quality Act, other Federal or State laws or executive orders may not contain such exemptions and require approval by one or more regulatory agencies. In some instances, emergency permits are available with expedited processing procedures, or regulatory agencies may allow the repair work to proceed while the permit(s) are being processed. Post-disaster recovery planning and procedures—addressing issues like preparation of a dredging plan, collecting sediment samples, laboratory analysis, and dredging and disposal—could be included in any future State guidance for maritime tsunami response and recovery.

Challenges in Rebuilding More Resiliently For a Historically Infrequent Hazard, Like Tsunami

Recent tsunamis in Chile and Japan have repeatedly shown that most structures receiving two or more meters of tsunami-induced flooding will likely be destroyed or need to be demolished. In this scenario, there will be pockets of catastrophic damage in communities all along the California coast.

Under NFIP, properties that are more than 50 percent damaged are supposed to have flood risk mitigation as part of rebuilding. Policies would need to be developed by State and local agencies to address standards for rebuilding areas of heavy damage as well as moderately damaged buildings and enforce the NFIP requirements for 50 percent or greater damaged structures. This may be politically challenging if tsunami resilient design standards have not yet been adopted as part of the CBC.

Local governments (for example, city and county) may be pressured to make less than 50 percent damage determinations so that people can rebuild to pre-disaster conditions. There may also be pressure to modify State and Federal policies and make exceptions for the tsunami disaster because tsunami has historically been a relatively infrequent hazard. The State TPHMP's plans to develop probabilistic tsunami hazard maps would provide an important resource to assist State and local agencies in managing post-disaster land-use planning, zoning, and rebuilding actions. Furthermore, creation of an official tsunami hazard zone under California's Seismic Hazard Mapping Act would also trigger tsunami design requirements for local post-disaster land use planning, zoning and rebuilding, including requirements for more site-specific investigation of associated geotechnical hazards and a plan to mitigate identified hazards before a building permit is issued. Local coastal counties and cities, as well as key reviewing and permitting agencies, such as the CCC, might need additional planning and technical assistance and guidelines to assist in implementing such an integrated mitigation policy framework post-disaster.

There could also be opportunities to advance multi-hazard mitigation planning post-disaster and address issues of future tsunami risk, sea level rise and future coastal flooding and erosion, and earthquake-induced liquefaction. Multi-hazard mitigation options could include relocation and redevelopment of buyout areas, structural elevations, or retrofitting of slab-on-grade foundations. Mitigation incentives could be provided through a variety of planning and recovery financing mechanisms. For example, California Assembly Bill 2140, passed in 2006, provides an option for the State to increase its part of the local match for FEMA Public Assistance grants that it provides to disaster-impacted counties and cities, if they have a FEMA-approved LHMP that has also been adopted (by reference or incorporation) into the safety element of their general plan. This requirement could be strengthened post-disaster and also linked with Local Coastal Plan requirements. The SAFRR tsunami scenario provides an opportunity for State agencies, including Cal OES, CGS, the CCC, and BCDC to explore where mitigation policies and programs for dealing with different hazards might be combined and strengthened.

Priority Policy Issues: Risk Awareness

An important function of risk awareness is to enhance the capacity of a person, household, or governmental unit to make informed resource allocation choices (Topping and others, 2010). As each becomes more aware of the tsunami risk that California faces, the greater the likelihood that they may decide to invest in resiliency actions.

This section presents three key policy issues: (1) building awareness of tsunami risk; (2) building constituencies that can carry a common message forward over time; and (3) educating and training key professionals working in engineering, planning, maritime industries, and emergency management along California's coast.

Building the Awareness of At-Risk Communities to Tsunami and Their Potential Damaging and Fatal Effects

Since the mid-1990s, California's emergency management community has been engaged in tsunami planning as part of multi-hazard planning. The catastrophic sequence of recent global tsunamis, starting with the December 26, 2004, Indian Ocean tsunami, have heightened tsunami risk awareness in the United States and California, and brought expanded funding to support the National Tsunami Hazard Mitigation Program as well as State and local tsunami emergency preparedness and public education programs.

The California Tsunami Steering Committee oversees the State's TPHMP, and its representatives come from all the coastal California counties, the NWS, and several State agencies. State program activities that are particularly focused on tsunami risk awareness include development and dissemination of outreach materials (brochures, pamphlets, DVDs), conducting educational workshops, supporting exercises and evacuation drills, participating in National Tsunami Preparedness Week, supporting regional work groups, purchasing tsunami hazard signs and developing tsunami sign placement plans, and coordinating with the NWS to support coastal communities in achieving TsunamiReady recognition. California currently leads the Nation in the number of communities (counties and cities) that have been recognized as TsunamiReady.

As the analyses for the SAFRR tsunami scenario have shown, however, there are significant gaps in tsunami risk awareness among the general public, at-risk populations, key responders, and State and local policymakers. Some key opportunities for building awareness, particularly of California's most at-risk populations include:

- Amending California's natural hazards disclosure law (California Civil Code sec. 1103 et seq.) to require that real-estate purchasers be notified by the seller or seller's agent when the property for sale is located in a tsunami hazard zone.
- Expanding "Tsunami Preparedness Week" to "Tsunami Preparedness Month." More time would allow for a more comprehensive public education and outreach program including school activities, fairs, town-hall meetings, evacuation exercises, live code tests of warning systems, and other special events.
- Expanding California's annual earthquake exercise and outreach effort known as the "Great California ShakeOut" to include tsunami education and preparedness in the program's goals and objectives, Web site, distributed material, and activities. Since its advent in 2008, California's ShakeOut program has dramatically increased community awareness and preparedness for earthquake hazards in California. In 2012, more than 9.4 million Californians registered for the Great California ShakeOut (Southern California Earthquake Center, 2013).
- Adding TsunamiReady awareness into the Great California ShakeOut activities.
- Promoting tsunami education and preparedness materials to hotel emergency coordinators who can share it with hotel guests.
- Ensuring that the "Risk Awareness" part of FEMA's Risk MAP (Mapping, Assessment, Planning) Program includes map-based information on tsunami risk. The Risk MAP theme to "clearly and effectively inform the public of their flood risk and impacts" exists but awaits implementation and

offers an opportunity to better link tsunami hazards into coastal flooding risks (see *http://www.fema.gov/library/viewRecord.do?id=3587*, accessed August 23, 2013).

Building Constituencies that can Carry a Common Message Forward Over Time is a Key Policy Challenge

Few of California's coastal communities, businesses, and residents have experienced a significant tsunami and understand, first hand, the risks. To raise risk awareness, there need to be constituencies that support clear and consistent messaging over the long-term.

Effective messaging needs to be consistent, unrelenting, and come from trusted sources (Topping and others, 2010). Most people respond better to graphic images than numerical data regarding risk and most also have difficulty dealing with probabilistic information; low probability events become "zero probability events" in people's minds (Daniels and others, 2006). The basic tsunami risk awareness message needs to resonate with the core survival values of at-risk local governments, special districts, businesses, residents along California's coast and stimulate them to advocate for action and take preparedness and mitigation actions themselves (for example, through training, obtaining insurance, knowing how to evacuate, having survival supplies at hand, and being able to communicate with local authorities following a disaster).

Such efforts especially need to focus on areas where the greatest chance of isolation might occur and making sure that neighbors are capable first responders to the event. This requires a variety of partnerships of awareness. Community-based disaster response training programs like Community Emergency Response Training (CERT) may be a good vehicle for risk awareness promotion and communication at the neighborhood level. Similar efforts within the maritime community also could be developed and promoted. The Redwood Coast Tsunami Work Group is a form of coalition building for a common tsunami hazard (see Redwood Coast Tsunami Work Group Facebook page, *accessed August 23, 2013* at *https://www.facebook.com/RCTWG?filter=3*) and a model that might be promoted in other regions of the State, such as the San Francisco Bay area, the central coast, and southern California.

The NTHMP provides a valuable multilevel coordination framework. Federal agencies working in partnership with the States and their communities to collect, interpret, and disseminate information on tsunami; promote public hazard awareness; and provide national, State, and local leadership and incentives to engage communities in tsunami preparedness and mitigation (for example TsunamiReady). For California's tsunami risk message to be delivered with one unified political voice (at a Federal, State, or regional level) sustained funding for the NTHMP and its State counterpart is needed, and some new programmatic efforts will be required. Champions may need to be developed among locally elected officials, possibly through the California League of Cities, the California State Association of Counties, the State Legislature, and California's Congressional delegation. West Coast States could also work as a coalition to advocate for sustained funding.

Educating the media (including media meteorologists) can also build pre-event alliances as part of the message delivery system. The Pacific Tsunami Warning Center has had some success in working with the media on tsunami risk awareness that may yield lessons for California (see *http://www.weather.gov/ptwc/*, accessed August 23, 2013).

Strengthening Tsunami Risk Awareness Among Key Professionals is Also a Key Policy Issue

Tsunami hazard assessment, and mitigation and response planning are still relatively "young" fields for engineering, emergency management, and scientists. Educational elements of the NTHMP and State TPHMP may need to be strengthened to reach key professionals working in engineering, as well as land-use, hazard mitigation, and response planning along California's coast.

In engineering, for example, college curriculums, licensing, and continuing education in coastal engineering, structural engineering, and civil engineering could include the broad topic of tsunami hazard, including source generation and propagation, hydrodynamic inundation modeling and its limitations, and sources and treatment of uncertainty. Similar curricula and continuing education might also be developed and promoted in college urban planning and emergency management programs across the State.

The maritime community also may need more focused training and education efforts. These might include incorporating a tsunami hazard component into harbor master guidebooks and ship-pilot licensing and boater-safety training programs. This might include information on basic tsunami characteristics, flow dynamics, the tsunami warning process, vessel evacuation procedures, designated harbor and offshore safety areas, and response planning for fuel, food, communications, and other supplies.

Possible Courses of Action

The SAFRR tsunami scenario aims to use science to inform decisions that enhance community resiliency, in this case resiliency against a tsunami that affects the entire West Coast of the United States. To actually enhance resiliency, however, significant disaster policy changes, programmatic adjustments, and organizational and individual behavioral adaptations will be required to face the immense challenges that such an extreme event poses. Some possible courses of actions that this assessment offers follow:

Ensure Continued Funding and Support for the National Tsunami Hazard Mitigation Program, TsunamiReady and Affiliated State and Local Programs

Federal funding for the NTHMP is scheduled to end in 2013. Unless the Tsunami Warning and Education Act of 2006 is reauthorized, the foundation of the Nation's and California's tsunami policy framework will be significantly diminished and the future of the TsunamiReady program, and State leadership for local tsunami hazard assessment, mitigation, and preparedness will be at significant risk.

Recruit and Assist All California Coastal Communities and Ports and Harbors to Become TsunamiReady

The TsunamiReady program, as a voluntary program, is more apt to attract better mitigation performers seeking this designation. Mechanisms are needed to encourage the most vulnerable and unprepared coastal communities and ports and harbors to voluntarily undertake mitigation and preparedness actions ahead of a tsunami disaster. The TsunamiReady program could help enhance communication, coordination, and information sharing among coastal communities on tsunami mitigation and preparedness plans and best practices. The standards for TsunamiReady designation might also be reviewed and a process for maintaining TsunamiReady designations over time might also be developed to help ensure that TsunamiReady designated communities and ports and harbors are indeed ready for the impacts of a future tsunami.

Develop a Coordinated and Sufficiently Robust Policy Framework for Tsunami Hazard Assessment and Mitigation Planning for California Coastal Communities and Ports and Harbors

A more robust and integrated planning framework would help to reinforce knowledge of hazards and their potential impacts, improve mitigation actions that could be taken to reduce vulnerability, and result in improved and more coordinated response efforts across all responsible government agencies during a disaster. Adoption of official State tsunami hazard zones under the State Seismic Hazard Mapping Act could provide a strong foundation for such an integrated framework. Guidelines could link the hazard zones into State and local land use, zoning, subdivision and development permitting processes as well as LHMPs, LCPs, and the safety elements of local general plans. Legislative changes may be needed to ensure better integration of the tsunami hazard zones in State and local planning and development requirements and consistency with any tsunami-resilient building design code provisions that are adopted. Similarly, consistent statewide guidelines for maritime tsunami response and recovery could be developed for use in harbor safety planning; evacuation, response and recovery planning by port, harbor and marina management; and pilot licensing and boater training programs.

Explore Opportunities to Advance Multi-Hazard Mitigation Planning Along California's Coast and Bays

The SAFRR tsunami scenario provides an opportunity to advance multi-hazard mitigation planning along California's coast and bays to more holistically address issues of future tsunami risk, sea-level rise and future coastal flooding and erosion, and earthquake-induced liquefaction. State agencies, including Cal OES, CGS, the CCC, and BCDC, could explore where mitigation policies and programs for dealing with different hazards might be combined and strengthened. Multi-hazard mitigation options could include relocation and redevelopment of buyout areas, structural elevations, or retrofitting of slab-on-grade foundations.

Encourage Responders and Government Managers to Conduct Self-Assessments, Devise Exercises, and More Carefully Consider the Geographic Scale of This and Other Tsunami Scenarios

Emergency responders and government managers at all levels could be encouraged to conduct self-assessments, devise exercises, and more carefully consider how the short-fuse intensity and wide geographic scale of the SAFRR and other tsunami scenarios could challenge current assumptions in warning and evacuation protocols, emergency response and planning documents, organizational structures and systems, and their abilities to scale up and meet the needs of such events and overcome the relative lack of experience that most managers and the general public will have with tsunami-specific issues. Such assessments and exercises could help to create more locally and regionally specific scenarios of impacts and also identify gaps in public and private sector resources available to respond to and recover from a large-scale tsunami. Political leaders, policymakers, and administrators could be involved in such assessments and exercises, and the level of emergency complexity and testing could be increased over time. An ongoing cycle of activities to account for normal staff turnover, provide refresher training, and update plans and operating procedures is needed to maintain an effective state of readiness. Tsunami evacuation "playbooks" under development by the State TPHMP will provide more detailed models of potential inundation areas for a number of different tsunami scenarios. Coastal emergency managers can then use them in preparing local evacuation response plans that are more tsunami source specific. Similarly, the State TPHMP maritime mapping and guidelines will help California's ports, harbors, and marinas to better plan for evacuations, response, and recovery. The SAFRR tsunami scenario provides important justification of the need for both the community playbooks and maritime planning products and the need for robust dissemination and training efforts associated with their release. The SAFRR tsunami scenario also provides a useful source of information to test national tsunami warning protocols and see what improvements could be made to alert dissemination protocols.

Work to Address Recovery Challenges

Work should be considered to address recovery challenges likely for the most vulnerable coastal communities and ports and harbors, as well parts of the State's fishing and agriculture sectors. The SAFFR tsunami scenario could also result in a fiscal crisis for coastal local governments and special districts struggling to meet the response and recovery needs of such a tsunami disaster, while simultaneously facing significant sales and property tax revenue reductions. This would be especially true in coastal communities that depend heavily on tourism, agricultural, and maritime activities impacted by the tsunami. The impacts could have cascading effects. All California coastal counties and cities could be encouraged to become participate communities in the National Flood Insurance Program. Similarly, NFIP coverage could be promoted to coastal residents and businesses to offer some additional protection from tsunami-induced flooding. Efforts could also be encouraged to streamline regulatory and permitting processes that would be required for port dredging and disposal and debris removal, both on- and offshore, after a tsunami disaster. Policies and programs may also be needed to address the removal of contaminated topsoil, desalinization of soils, and the detoxification of concrete and other affected building materials.

Develop and Consistently Communicate Common Messages About Tsunami Risk

It is essential to develop and consistently communicate common messages to educate the general public, at-risk populations, and businesses, State and local policymakers, and key professionals about tsunami risk. Federal, State, and local models exist for crafting and executing a robust tsunami risk awareness and education program for a major tsunami striking California and the rest of the West Coast. Multilevel, multifactor involvement needs to be a core component of such an effort. Opportunities for building awareness, particularly of California's most at-risk populations, include amending California's natural hazards disclosure law (California Civil Code sec. 1103 et seq.) to require that real estate purchasers be notified by the seller or seller's agent when the property for sale is located in a tsunami hazard zone and expanding California's annual earthquake exercise and outreach effort known as "ShakeOut" to include tsunami education and preparedness. Because tsunami hazard assessment, and mitigation and response planning are still relatively "young" fields tsunami education and training needs to be strengthened to reach key professionals working in engineering, as well as land-use, hazard mitigation, and response planning along California's coast.

References Cited

American Society of Civil Engineers, 2013, Academy of coastal, ocean, port and navigation engineers: American Society of Civil Engineers Web site, accessed August 26, 2013, at http://www.asce.org/Certification/Academy-of-Coastal,-Ocean,-Port---Navigation-Engineers/.

Birkland, T., 1997, After disaster—Agenda setting, public policy, and focusing events: Washington D.C., Georgetown University Press, 192 p.

Birkland, T., 2006, Lessons of disaster—Policy change after catastrophic events, Washington, D.C.: Georgetown University Press.

Borrero, J., Dengler, L., Burak, U., and Synolakis, C., 2006, Numerical modeling of tsunami effects at marine oil terminals in San Francisco Bay: California State Lands Commission, Marine Facilities Division, accessed August 26, 2013, at

http://www.google.com/url?sa=t&rct=j&q=&esrc=s&source=web&cd=1&ved=0CC8QFjAA&url=htt
p%3A%2F%2Fwww.slc.ca.gov%2Fdivision_pages%2Fmfd%2Fmotems%2Fsftsunamireport%2Fsf_
mot_final_report.doc&ei=nOTHUb_1DqiQigKylYDoBg&usg=AFQjCNGFCI2LjjoUqD10Myi70iN
VfnGEiQ&sig2=mEATGbNHGyxN1-8ADi6qNg&bvm=bv.48293060,d.cGE.

California State Lands Commission, 2013, About us—Land leasing: California State Lands
Commission Web site, accessed August 26, 2013, at
http://www.slc.ca.gov/About_The_CSLC/Land_Leasing.html.

California Building Standards Commission, 2010, 2010 California building code, title 24, v. 1 of part 2:
California Building Standards Commission, accessed August 26, 2013, at
http://publicecodes.cyberregs.com/st/ca/st/b200v10/st_ca_st_b200v10_intro.htm.

Daniels, R., Kettl, D., and Kunreuther, H., ed., 2006, On risk and disaster—Lessons from hurricane
Katrina: Philadelphia, University of Pennsylvania Press, 293 p.

Federal Emergency Management Agency [FEMA], 2005, Disaster assistance—A guide to recovery
programs, FEMA 229(4): Washington, D.C., Federal Emergency Management Agency, accessed
August 26, 2013, at http://www.fema.gov/txt/rebuild/ltrc/recoveryprograms229.txt.

Federal Emergency Management Agency [FEMA], 2007, Robert T. Stafford Disaster Relief And
Emergency Assistance Act, as amended, and related authorities, FEMA 592: Washington, D.C.,
Federal Emergency Management Agency, 113 p.

Federal Emergency Management Agency [FEMA], 2008, National response framework: Washington,
D.C., Federal Emergency Management Agency Web site, accessed August 26, 2013, at
http://www.fema.gov/national-response-framework.

Federal Emergency Management Agency [FEMA], 2011, National disaster recovery framework—
Strengthening disaster recovery for the Nation: Washington, D.C., Federal Emergency Management
Agency, accessed August 26, 2013, at http://www.fema.gov/pdf/recoveryframework/ndrf.pdf.

Federal Emergency Management Agency [FEMA], 2012a, Multi-hazard mitigation planning:
FEMA.gov, http://www.fema.gov/multi-hazard-mitigation-planning.

Federal Emergency Management Agency [FEMA], 2012b, Preparedness: Washington, D.C., Federal
Emergency Management Agency Web site, accessed August 26, 2013, at
http://www.fema.gov/preparedness-0#item1.

Federal Emergency Management Agency [FEMA], 2013, National response framework: Washington
D.C., Federal Emergency Management Agency, Web site, accessed August 26, 2013, at
http://www.fema.gov/library/viewRecord.do?id=7371.

Kirby, S., Scholl, D., Huene, R.V., and Wells, R., 2013, Alaska earthquake source for the SAFRR
California tsunami scenario: U.S. Geological Survey Open-File Report 2013–1170–B, 45 p.,
http://pubs.usgs.gov/of/2013/1170/b/.

May, P.J., and Williams, W., 1986. Disaster policy implementation—Managing programs under shared
governance: New York, N.Y., Plenum Press, 210 p.

Moffatt and Nichol, 2012, Tsunami scenario engineering impacts of Port of Long Beach and Port of Los
Angeles: Moffatt and Nichol report prepared for the U.S. Geological Survey, 51 p.

National Oceanic and Atmospheric Administration [NOAA], 2013a, About the national tsunami hazard
mitigation program: National Oceanic and Atmospheric Administration, National Tsunami Hazard
Mitigation Program Web site, accessed August 26, 2013, at
http://nthmp.tsunami.gov/about_program.html.

National Oceanic and Atmospheric Admistration, [NOAA], 2013b, California—36 TsunamiReady sites:
National Oceanic and Atmospheric Administration, TsunamiReady Web site, accessed August 26,
2013, at http://www.tsunamiready.noaa.gov/ts-com/ca-ts.htm.

National Research Council, 2011, Tsunami warning and preparedness—An assessment of the U.S. tsunami program and the Nation's preparedness efforts: Washington D.C., The National Academies Press, 284 p.

Newell, C., ed. 2004, The Effective Local Government Manager, 3rd ed: Washington, D.C., International City/County Management Association, Municipal Management Series, 267 p.

Olshansky, R.B., Hopkins, L.D., and Johnson, L.A., 2012, Disaster and recovery—Processes compressed in time: Natural Hazards Review, v. 13, no. 3, p. 173–178, doi:10.1061/(ASCE)NH.1527-6996.0000077.

Plumlee, G.S., Morman, S.A., and San Juan, C., 2013, Potential environmental and environmental-health implications of the SAFRR California tsunami scenario: U.S. Geological Survey Open-File Report 2013–1170–F, 39 p., http://pubs.usgs.gov/of/2013/1170/f/.

Porter, K., Byers, W., Dykstra, D., Lim, A., Lynett, P., Ratliff, J., Scawthorn, C., Wein, A., and Wilson, R., 2013, Physical damage in the SAFRR California tsunami scenario: U.S. Geological Survey Open-File Report 2013–1170–E, 183 p., http://pubs.usgs.gov/of/2013/1170/E/.

Rubin, C., 2012, Emergency management—The American experience 1900–2010, 2nd ed.: Boca Raton, Fla., CRC Press, Taylor and Francis Group, 303 p.

Southern California Earthquake Center, 2013, The great California shakeout—Check the Stats: Southern California Earthquake Center, Web site, accessed August 26, 2013, at http://www.shakeout.org/california/.

State of California, 2005, California code of regulations, title 14, division 1, subdivision 4, chapter 3: State of California Web site, accessed August 26, 2013, at https://nrm.dfg.ca.gov/FileHandler.ashx?DocumentID=21888&inline=true.

State of California, 2009, Tsunami inundation maps for emergency planning: State of California, Department of Conservation, Web site, accessed August 26, 2013, at http://www.conservation.ca.gov/cgs/geologic_hazards/Tsunami/Inundation_Maps/Pages/Statewide_Maps.aspx.

Topping, K.C., Johnson, L.A., Eadie, C.C., and Siembieda, W., 2010, Public policy issues, *in* Overview of the ARkStorm scenario: U.S. Geological Survey Open-File Report 2010-1312, http://pubs.usgs.gov/of/2010/1312/.

U.S. Congress, House and Senate Appropriations Committees, 2005, Emergency supplemental appropriations act for defense—The Global War on Terror, and tsunami relief: U.S. Government Printing Office, U.S. Congress, 109th, Public Law 13, accessed August 26, 2013, at http://www.gpo.gov/fdsys/pkg/PLAW-109publ13/html/PLAW-109publ13.htm.

U.S. Congress, House Science, Space, and Technology Committee, 2006, Tsunami Warning and Education Act: U.S. Congress, 109th, H.R. 109-698, accessed August 26, 2013, at http://beta.congress.gov/congressional-report/109th-congress/house-report/698/1.

Uslu, B., Borrero, J., Dengler, L., Synolakis, C., and Barberopoulou, A., 2008, Tsunami inundation from great earthquakes on the Cascadia subduction zone along the northern California coast, *in* Wallendorf, L., Ewing L., Jones, C., and Jaffe, B., eds., Solutions to coastal disasters 2008: American Society of Civil Engineers, p. 204–214.

Uslu, B., Eble, M., Titov, V.V., and Bernard, E.N., 2010, Distant tsunami threats to the ports of Los Angeles and Long Beach, California: National Oceanic and Atmospheric Administration, Office of Oceanic and Atmospheric Research Special Report, Tsunami Hazard Assessment Special Series, v. 2, 111 p., accessed August 26, 2013, at http://nctr.pmel.noaa.gov/hazard_assessment_reports/02_LA_LB_CA_3532_web.pdf.

Wein, A., Rose, A., Sue Wing, I., Wei, D., 2013, Economic impacts of the SAFRR tsunami scenario in California: U.S. Geological Survey Open-File Report 2013–1170–H, 56 p., http://pubs.usgs.gov/of/2013/1170/h/.

Wilson, R., and Miller, K., 2013, Tsunami mitigation and preparedness activities in California: U.S. Geological Survey Open-File Report 2013–1170–L, 10 p., http://pubs.usgs.gov/of/2013/1170/l/.

Wood, N., Ratliff, J., Peters, J., and Shoaf, K., 2013, Population vulnerability and evacuation challenges in California for the SAFRR tsunami scenario: U.S. Geological Survey Open-File Report 2013–1170–I, 53 p., http://pubs.usgs.gov/of/2013/1170/i/.